The Family of Cato West

Acting Governor of the Mississippi Territory 1804–1805

on the

Bicentenary
of
His Death

by

Alycon Trubey Pierce, CG[SM]

HERITAGE BOOKS
2019

HERITAGE BOOKS

AN IMPRINT OF HERITAGE BOOKS, INC.

Books, CDs, and more—Worldwide

For our listing of thousands of titles see our website
at
www.HeritageBooks.com

Published 2019 by
HERITAGE BOOKS, INC.
Publishing Division
5810 Ruatan Street
Berwyn Heights, Md. 20740

Heritage Books by the author:

Daniel Trubey of Franklin County, Pennsylvania: The First Four Generations

*Selected Final [Revolutionary] Pension Payment Vouchers 1818–1864:
Alabama: Decatur—Huntsville—Mobile—Tuscaloosa*

Selected Final Pension Payment Vouchers, 1818–1864: District of Columbia

Selected Final Pension Payment Vouchers, 1818–1864: Maryland: Baltimore

*Selected Final Pension Payment Vouchers, 1818–1864: New Jersey: Trenton
(Two-Volume Set: A-M and N-Z)*

*The Family of Cato West, Acting Governor of the Mississippi Territory, 1804–1805,
on the Bicentenary of His Death*

Cover illustration: Melish, John. *Map of Mississippi: constructed from the surveys in the
General Land Office and other documents.* [Philadelphia: J. Melish, 1820] Map.
Retrieved from the Library of Congress, <www.loc.gov/item/2001626031/>.

International Standard Book Number
Paperbound: 978-0-7884-5702-9

Contents

Preface

To rephrase the reported exchange between F. Scott Fitzgerald and Ernest Hemingway: "The rich are different from you and me." "Yes, they *leave more records*."

Cato West was one such rich man. Yet, despite West's high political profile and record trail, his personal history and family details are often poorly documented. This publication provides a brief summary of documentation on his parents and paternal grandparents, but focuses upon Cato West, his brother, wives, children, grandchildren, and, in some instances, great-grandchildren.

This research on Cato West began in the 1980s, when this author noted that Cato's grandson Rev. James Raiford West (b.1805) resided contemporaneously in the same Holmes County, Mississippi, neighborhood with the author's elusive ancestress Ann Eliza (James) Watson (b.1830-d.1851), who named her firstborn son "James Raiford" Watson. No blood connection has been found between Ann Eliza James and the West (or Raiford) family, and her ancestry remains undocumented.

However, researching their possible kinship uncovered extensive documentary evidence and detail on Cato West, some of which contradicted published and posted assertions about Cato West's birthplace, birth date, parents, siblings, wives, and children. For that reason, this compilation was undertaken to present the facts of Cato West and his family that emerged from cited documentary evidence. Not coincidentally, the publication of this genealogy falls on the bicentenary of Cato West's 1819 death in Jefferson County, Mississippi.

Mississippi chancery courts' probate packets for many members of the West family provide detailed and varied evidence for those then living as well as for the dead: the ordinary purchases of a privileged family; minors reaching their majority; names, ages, births, and deaths of the enslaved; schooling away from home; and tensions stemming from step-relatives. Only six of Cato's fifteen children by two wives left descendants beyond grandchildren, but correlating the existing documentation made it possible to present a fuller portrait of each of the fifteen, especially of his childless offspring, than often is possible or typically provided in published genealogies. Providing fuller genealogies for each child serves to nail down their identities and stem the confusion that heretofore has plagued Cato West researchers.

Research on the family of Cato West includes documentation originally accessed on microfilm at the Family History Library in Salt Lake City, Utah. While digitized images of some of the same records are now available, the citations herein continue to reference the FHL microfilm numbers. The reader can access the available digital images through FamilySearch's "Catalog" option by entering the microfilm number under "Film/Fiche Number," and then selecting the camera icon for that microfilm.

Some cited web addresses, or URLs, are no longer operational but the websites they once led to may yet be accessed by entering the old URL into the Internet Archive's "Wayback Machine."

All U.S. census citations refer to population schedules unless otherwise noted. All newspaper notices were viewed at *Chronicling America.loc.gov*, *GenealogyBank.com*, *Newspapers.com*, or *NewspaperArchive.com* unless otherwise noted.

Special thanks go to Candace Bundgard, Robert de Berardinis, John Fishback, Barbara Vines Little, CG[SM], Joan W. Peters, and Craig Roberts Scott, CG[SM]. Thanks also to the staff and archivists of The Historic New Orleans Collection; West Florida University; (J. M. Duffin) University of Pennsylvania Archives and Records Center; National Archives, Washington and Atlanta; Bureau of Land Management; and the state archives of Mississippi, North Carolina, South Carolina, and Virginia. The generous involvement of librarians, curators, collection managers, and other researchers in providing historical documents helped illuminate the lives of Cato West's greater family.

Alycon Trubey Pierce, CG[SM]
Falls Church, Virginia
2019

The Family of Cato West
Acting Governor of the Mississippi Territory 1804-1805

Cato West left his native Virginia as a young man around the time of the American Revolution, serving briefly in South Carolina before resigning his commission. Soon thereafter he married and travelled with his wife's family to Natchez in Spanish West Florida, later the Mississippi Territory, where his political ambitions flourished. Thomas Jefferson nominated, and Congress confirmed, West as Treasurer of the Mississippi Territory in 1803. After Jefferson sent Mississippi Territorial Governor William C. C. Claiborne to New Orleans to oversee the transfer of the Louisiana Territory into U.S. possession in 1803, Cato West became the acting interim governor of the Mississippi Territory from 1804 to 1805. The historical record catalogues his political activities up to his death in 1819, but his reconstructed genealogical connections are often incorrect. The information that follows presents Cato West's nearest genealogical forebears and progeny as revealed by documentation contemporary to those individuals.

Paternal Grandparents of Cato West

1. WILLIAM[1] WEST was born about 1714,[1] and had several children with ELIZABETH GARDNER before they married about 1741-1742.[2] Elizabeth died sometime before 17 October 1761, when William obtained a license in Loudoun County, Virginia, to marry MARY "POLLY" ELLZEY.[3] No children are known from this second marriage, which lasted until William's death in 1769.[4]

William West left a lengthy will:

> In the name of God, Amen, I William West of Loudoun County Being in sound mind health and memory and call Into mind the uncertainty of this mortal life I do hereby appoint this my last will and testament in manner and form following to dispose of the

---

[1] Assumes he was about age twenty-two when eldest child Elizabeth was born about 1736 (Loudoun Co., Va., Deed Book U:315–17, depositions of Mary Gardner and Ann Botts, 4 May 1772; FHL microfilm 32,306). For documentation of the parentage and life of William West (d.1769), see Jim Bish's "The Importance of William West, His Fruit Hill Ordinary, and His Family in the Development of Loudoun County," *The Bulletin of the Loudoun County Historical Society*, v.2008-2009, 33-40. See also Alycon Trubey Pierce, CG, "Slave Records Correct Cato West's Confused Ancestry," *National Genealogical Society Quarterly,* v.99, no.1 (March 2011): 5-14.
[2] Ibid. In addition to this William West and his eldest son of the same name, a third William West resided or at least died in Loudoun County in the mid-1700s: "Last Monday se'nnight [seven days and nights ago] died in Loudoun county, Capt. William West, a Gentleman who was extremely serviceable in the last Indian war, and whose death is lamented by all his acquaintances, especially the poor, to whom he was a friend and physician"; Robert K. Headley, Jr., *Genealogical Abstracts from 18th-Century Virginia Newspapers* (Baltimore: Genealogical Publishing Co., Inc., 1987), 362, citing Rind's *Virginia Gazette,* 19 October 1761 supplement.
[3] Mary Alice Wertz, *Marriages of Loudoun County, Virginia, 1757-1853* (Baltimore: Clearfield – Genealogical Publishing Co., 1985), 164, citing the "Loudoun County Clerk's 1761 Fee Book no. 4, in the custody of the Loudoun Museum," but that volume has not been located there or in the courthouse.
[4] Loudoun County, Virginia, oversized original will of William West (Sr.), 26 June 1769, proved 13 November 1769; Circuit Court Archives, Leesburg, Va. Recorded in Will Book A:226; FHL microfilm 32,275.

worldly goods that god hath blest me with after my just debts is paid in prims I give and Bequeath to my loving wife Mary West the following Negroes (Viz.) Pug, Hannah, Tom, Nace, and James and also the use of the Land and plantation whereon I now Live during her Natural Life also the Stock and household Furniture Except hereafter Excepted as also the use of one Negro boy named Tom Tomson—During her Natural Life which Negro Boy Land and house household furniture and stock shall after her death return to my heirs according to the Bequeaths hereafter mentioned Item I give and bequeath to my son Charles all that part of my Land Beginning at John Hall's red oak Corner Standing on Roger's is Spring Branch near the new road then with Straight Line to said road and Binding therewith to the first fork of Bull run where the said road Crosses then up the sd Northernmost branch to the Back Line Including the house wherein Isaac Betzell now Lives Near the said branch, as also Henry Landers and where the [page 227] Said Charles West now Lives all the Land first mentioned Line to the road and all the Land Joining John Evines Robert Carter and John Hall Being the North part of my tract of Land to him and to his heirs for ever Provided he the said Charles West Shall pay yearly to his Brother John West the sum of ten pounds During the Natural life of Said John West and Failure of the yearly payment of the said sum by the said Charles West or his heirs or any Claiming the said Land my will and Desire is that he the said John West shall have and hold one half of the Said Land as my will and Bequeath to him -- Also I give to my Son Charles West one Negro man Named Jack one negro Woman named Leah, one Negro man named Congo, one Negro Woman Named mariah as also all the household -- Furniture That he has in his hands (Except one Bed). Item, I give and bequeath to my son Charles West that tract of Land in Loudoun County called Baconfort (viz.) to him his heirs for ever. Item I give and Bequeath to my son Thomas West the remainder of my tract of Land Joining his Brother Charles West, to the said first branch of Bullrun where the road Crosses then down the said run as my bounds now stands Including Garret Snedekar and Charles Morris being the Easterly part of the tract to him and his heirs for ever. Provided he the said Thomas West shall pay yearly to his Brother John West the sum of five pounds During the Natural Life of the said John West and on Failure of the yearly payment of the Said Sum by the sd Thomas West or his heirs or any Claiming the sd Land my will and Desire is that he ye said John West shall have and hold one half of the said Land as my will and Bequeath to him, also I Bequeath to my son Thomas West one Negro man Named Dick and one Negro man Named Melford, also one Feather Bed and Furniture in hand of Charles West. Item I give and Bequeath to my two grand Sons Cato West and Charles West all my Land Laying on the South Side of the North fork of Bull run joining my Son Charles West being part in Prince William and part in Loudoun Counties Including the plantations where John Alison [page 228] and Simon Simeson and Moses Lasswell now Live to be Equally Divided Between them to them and to their heirs for ever and in Default of Such heirs then the said to my Son Charles West as also two Cows and Calves one Feather bed to Each of them to be paid at the age Eighteen years if required this I leave in Full bar against any Claim or Claims that they or Either of them Shall have or Demand or any other person for them against the Estate of their Deceased Father William West and of any such Claim shall be made by them or any other person for them then in that Case I will the said gifts and Bequeaths to be Sold or So much as will pay the said Legacies and all Charges. Item I give and Bequeath unto my grand Daughter Elizabeth West the Daughter of Charles West and Anne his Wife one Negro girl named Heinne to her and her heirs for ever. Item I give and Bequeath to my Daughter Anne Peyton one Negro Woman named Sarah. Item I give and Bequeath to my grand Son William Peyton my Lott and house thereon in Leesburgh (viz.) to him and his heirs for ever. Item I give and Bequeath to my grand Daughter Margaret Peyton one Negro girl named Sib. Item I give and Bequeath to my grand Son Francis Peyton one

2

Negro girl Named Phebe. Item I give and Bequeath to my grand Son Craven Peyton one Negro girl Named Dalilah. Item I give and Bequeath to my grand Daughter Elizabeth West the Daughter of Charles West and Anne his Wife my Land in Fairfax County Laying on the Ox Road to her and her heirs for ever. Item I give and Bequeath to my Daughter Anne Peyton the afforesaid [*sic*] Negro Boy named Tom Tomson after the Marriage or Decease of my said Wife (but She my Said Wife to have the use of all the before mentioned to her During her Natural Life or widowhood). But at the time She Shall marry or Depart this Life then all that is Bequeathed to her shall be Equally Divided between three of my Children (viz.) Charles West, Thomas West, and [page 229] Anne Peyton Except the first five mentioned Negroes (viz.) Pug, Tom, Hannah, Nace and James which Negroes I give to her and to her Disposal. And I do hereby appoint my Wife and Charles West and Craven Peyton to be my Executors of this my last will and Testament. Whereunto I have set my hand fixed my seal this twenty six Day of June Anoq. 1769
Signed cealed [*sic*] and Delivered
In Presents [*sic*] of
John Hall[,] Bety [x her mark] Hall   WWest {seal}[5]
Robert Hamilton[,] Wm Baker

The widowed Mary (Ellzey) West—stepgrandmother of Cato West—wrote her will in 1777 that was only "partially proven" in Loudoun County and did not mention any of the Wests.[6]

The children of William[1] West Sr. and Elizabeth Gardner:

    i.   ELIZABETH[2] WEST, born possibly in Fairfax County, Virginia, about 1736.[7]

2. ii.   WILLIAM WEST JR., born probably in Fairfax Co., about 1738; married Mary Winn about 1757, Loudoun Co., Va.; died before 12 April 1763, Loudoun Co.

    iii.   JOHN WEST, born probably in Fairfax Co., about 1741-1742.[8]

    iv.   ANNE WEST, born probably in Fairfax Co., about 1742; married Craven Peyton.[9]

    v.   CHARLES WEST, born probably in Fairfax Co., about 1743-1745; married Anne [—?—].[10]

    vi.   THOMAS WEST, born probably in Fairfax Co., about 1750; died by 13 January 1777, Loudoun Co.[11]

---

[5] Ibid.

[6] Loudoun Co., Va., Partially Proven Wills and Deeds 1:10075, will of Mary West, 15 May 1777, proved 12 September 1803; Circuit Court Archives, Leesburg. Lewis Ellzey mentioned his daughter Mary (Ellzey) West in his will (Fairfax Co., Va., Will Book E:223, 1 October 1785, proved 19 December 1786; LVA Fairfax Co. microfilm reel 28).

[7] Loudoun Co., Va., Deed Book U:315–17, depositions of Mary Gardner and Ann Botts, 4 May 1772.

[8] Loudoun Co., Va., Will Book A:226, will of William West (Sr.), 26 June 1769, proved 13 November 1769. John was at least age sixteen when he appeared with his father in Loudoun County's first tithable list in 1758; *FamilySearch* (www.familysearch.org), "List of Tithables, 1758-1799," Loudoun County, 1758, Francis Peyton's list, image 8, William West, John West; FHL microfilm 31,052.

[9] The wills of her father (A:226) and her husband (B:378) identify the same first four of her Peyton children. Loudoun Co., Va., Will Book B:378-381, will of Craven Peyton, 30 October 1780, proved 26 August 1776; FHL microfilm 32,275.

[10] Loudoun Co., Va., Chancery Case M2993, West v. West, file 1786-011, 14 June 1771; Circuit Court Archives, Leesburg.

[11] The 1772 Gardner and Botts depositions do not mention William and Elizabeth's son Thomas when identifying the children born before and after the parents' marriage, so the order of Thomas's birth is not indicated. However,

Parents of Cato West

2. WILLIAM[2] WEST, JR. (*William[1]*), son of William West and Elizabeth Gardner, was born about 1738,[12] probably in Fairfax County, Virginia. He was married about 1757, the year Loudoun County was formed from Fairfax County, to MARY "POLLY" WINN (daughter of Minor Winn),[13] who was likely born about 1740. When about age twenty-four, William penned a brief last will and testament on 15 November 1762:

> In the Name of God, Amen, I, Wm. West of Loudoun county do appoint this my Last Will as followeth—I give to my two sons Cato and Charles my whole Estate when they shall be of age my Wife to be maintained out of the said Estate as long as they think proper and the said Estate equally divided between the said Cato and Charles. I leave Craven Peyton and Charles West my Exrs of this my last Will and Testament and trusting in the Merits of Christ to save my Soul I hereunto set my hand this 15th Novr. 1762.
> Wm. West Junr.
>
> Witness
> WWest, John Hall, William Atterbury[14]

The executors William designated in his will refused to take on the "Burden of the Execution thereof"; the widowed Mary (Winn) West "refused to accept of the provisions made for her in the said Will" and she was granted "letters of administration with the will annexed."[15] Two years later, in February 1765, John Smith and the widow Mary West obtained a marriage license in Loudoun County.[16] Mary's father Minor Winn died testate in 1775, leaving a will that identifies her as "Mary Smith."[17] Her second husband John Smith died intestate in Fauquier County before 22 July 1782, when Mary was bonded as administratrix of his estate.[18] Both of their sons, John and Richard Smith, were of age to select their own guardians in 1784 and 1785.[19]

Thomas first appears on tithable lists in 1767, having reached age sixteen, which places his birth about 1750; *FamilySearch* (www.familysearch.org), "List of Tithables, 1758-1799," Loudoun County, 1767, Capt. John Moss Junr.'s list, image 171, Craven Peyton, Thos. West; FHL microfilm 31,052. That comports with Thomas's reaching legal age of twenty-one in 1771 when he served as guardian, "for this purpose specially appointed" (ad litem), of minor nephew Cato per brother Charles West's chancery case (Loudoun County, Va., Chancery Case M2993, West v. West, file 1786-011). Loudoun Co., Va., Will Book B:142-143, will of Thomas West, 26 August 1776, proved 13 January 1777; FHL microfilm 32,275.

[12] Mary Gardner deposition states William West Jr. (and John West) born before their parents married about 1741-1742 (Loudoun Co., Va., Deed Book U:316).

[13] Fauquier Co., Va., Will Book 1:343, will of Minor Winn, 31 July 1775, proved 23 March 1778; FHL microfilm 31,566. Minor's bequest to daughter Mary "Smith" refers to William West Jr.'s remarried widow.

[14] Loudoun Co., Va., Will Book A:73, will of William West Jr., 15 November 1762, proved 12 April 1763; FHL microfilm 32,275.

[15] Ibid.

[16] Loudoun Co., Va., Fee Book 1765, "Account of Ordinary Licences &c," marriage bond of John Smith and Mary West Widow, £1.0.0, February 1765, C. Binns; County Clerk's Office, Leesburg.

[17] Fauquier Co., Va., Will Book 1:343, will of Minor Winn, 31 July 1775, proved 23 March 1778.

[18] Fauquier Co., Va., Mary Smith bond as administratrix of John Smith's estate, with Peter Grant, Minor Winn, and Burr Hamilton securities for £1,000; Clerk of the Circuit Court, document 1782-014.

[19] Fauquier Co., Va., Minute Book 1781-1784, 283, John Smith chose Peter Grant as his guardian, April court 1784; FHL microfilm 31,614. Fauquier Co., Va., Minute Book 1784-1786, 244, Richard Smith chose Minor Winn as his guardian, September court 1785; FHL microfilm 31,615.

John Smith's estate records show that Mary married a third time, two months after she began administering John's estate, to Nathaniel Weedon per bond recorded on 18 September 1782 in Fauquier County.[20] The couple resided in adjacent Loudoun County, where the 1784 tithable list recorded jointly Nathaniel Weedon and Charles West (Mary's second son by her first husband).[21] In rapid succession, Nathaniel Weedon sold his Loudoun County property,[22] and relocated the family to Frederick County, Virginia, 1787-1791,[23] then to Fayette County, Kentucky, 1792-1795,[24] to Clark County, Kentucky, 1796-1797,[25] and to Jessamine County, Kentucky, in 1800.[26] Family problems had surfaced in 1792, when Weedon placed the following warning in the Lexington newspaper involving his stepson and wife:

> Fifty Dollars Reward – Whereas a certain Richard Smith hath by some unlawful means got into his possession (about the tenth of May last) two Negroes, one a boy about 16 or 17 years of age, well made flat nose, slow motion, has lately had the small pox; the other a girl about 13 or 14 years old, smart and active but rather small for her age; these negroes being my property, I will give the above reward to any person who will deliver them to me at Mastersons station near Lexington, and forewarn all persons from purchasing said negroes or transporting them out of this State either by land or water, as they shall answer the same at their peril—I further forewarn all persons from crediting or in any wise bargaining or contracting with my wife Mary, without my consent in writing. Nathaniel Weedon. June 8th 1792.[27]

Mary "Polly" (Winn) West Smith Weedon moved from Kentucky and resided in the Mississippi Territory at the time of her death in 1809:

> Obituary
> All, all on earth is shadow; all beyond is substance...How solid all, where change shall be no more

---

[20] Fauquier Co., Va., Will Book 2 (1783-1795), 53, administration account, 28 April 1784, "1783 Feby 10th, The estate of John Smith Dec'd Dr. to Nathaniel Weedon who married the widow of sd Smith...," FHL microfilm 31,566. Fauquier Co., Va., Marriage Bond Transcriptions, 121, Nathaniel Weedon and Mary Smith widow, 18 September 1782, Bondsman Charles West (Mary's former brother-in-law or son); FHL microfilm 31,633.
[21] *FamilySearch* (www.familysearch.org), "List of Tithables, 1758-1799," Loudoun County, 1784, John Alexander's list, image 849, Nathaniel Wedin, Charles West; FHL microfilm 31,052.
[22] *The Virginia Journal and Alexandria Advertiser*, 13 October 1785, v.2, issue 29, page not given, "To be sold at private Sale, any Time before the first Day of December next, when Possession will be given..." 150 acres in "Loudon" [sic] County on Little River, within 45 miles of Alexandria and about 40 from Dumfries with elegant stone house...mill house...storehouse...stills...The Subscriber has also for sale, three hundred and ten acres of leased land, nearly all tillable.... Any person inclinable to purchase, may apply to the Subscriber on the premises. Nathaniel Weedon. October 4, 1785."
[23] Frederick Co., Va., Court Order Book 20:535, Nathaniel Weedon sworn constable, September 1787; FHL microfilm 31,425, and Court Order Book 23:52, Nathaniel and Mary Weedon vs. Henry, Richard, and Wade Hampton, March 1791; FHL microfilm 31,427. Frederick County, Winchester Town, Personal Property Tax Lists, Nathaniel Weedon, 23 March 1787, 3 April 1788, 30 April 1789; FHL microfilm 1,905,764, item 2.
[24] Fayette Co., Kentucky, Tax Lists 1792:23; 1793:19; 1794:18; 1795:14, Nathaniel Weaden; FHL microfilm 2,110,987.
[25] Clark Co., Kentucky, Tax Books 1796, List 2:27, and 1797, List 1:18, Nathaniel Weedon, no real property; FHL microfilm 7,930.
[26] Jessamine Co., Kentucky, Tax Book 1800:36, Nath'l Weeden; FHL microfilm 8,084.
[27] *Kentucky Gazette* (Lexington), Saturday, 9 June 1792, v.5, no.39, p.3, col.3. Image of this page available online (http://nyx.uky.edu/dips/xt7hdr2p669k/data/0382.pdf).

Departed this life on Wednesday the 6th of September, in Jefferson County, M. T., after a long & painful indisposition Mrs. Polly Weeden, mother of Col. Cato West.[28]

The children of William[2] West Jr. and Mary Winn:

3.   i.   CATO[3] WEST, born 1751-1758 in Fairfax or Loudoun Co., Va; married (1) Martha Wills Green about 1780, (2) Martha Harper 1810 in Jefferson Co., M.T.; died January 1819 Jefferson Co., Miss.

4.   ii.   CHARLES WEST, born 1751-1761 in Fairfax or Loudoun Co., Va.; married Sarah Withers on or after 10 June 1785 in Fauquier Co., Va.; died before 17 September 1795, Natchez, Mississippi Territory.

Cato West

3. CATO[3] WEST (*William[2, 1]*), son of William West Jr. and Mary Winn,[29] was born sometime between 1751 and 1758[30] in the area of Fairfax County that in 1757 became Loudoun County.[31] His father, William West Jr., wrote a will on 15 November 1762, mentioning his unnamed wife and two sons Cato and Charles.[32] Cato and Charles West's names appear in this same order in their grandfather William West Sr.'s 1769 will[33] and in the sole guardianship record their uncle Charles West[34] filed for them in Loudoun County on 29 September 1772,[35] suggesting that Cato was the older brother. Guardian and uncle Charles West's 1771 chancery suit, brought against his brother John West and nephew Cato West, stated that Cato was the "eldest [*sic*] son and heir at law" of their late brother William West Jr.[36] Cato West and his brother Charles represent the only males to perpetuate their grandfather's West line,[37] and both left Virginia before 1795. Both brothers would end their days as men of note in Mississippi.

---

[28] *Weekly Chronicle* (Natchez, Miss. Terr.), 16 September 1809, p.3, col.2.

[29] This author's research, published in the *National Genealogical Society Quarterly* (99 [March 2011]: 5-14), documented Cato West's parents as well as his paternal grandparents (William West Sr. and Elizabeth Gardner), and maternal grandfather (Minor Winn).

[30] The 1771 chancery case involving Cato and his uncles specified Cato was then under age twenty-one; Loudoun Co., Va., Chancery Case M2993 (Charles West v. John West, etc., 1786-011), 14 June 1771; images available at the Library of Virginia's "Chancery Records Index" site (https://www.lva.virginia.gov/chancery/case_detail.asp?CFN=107-1786-011). See also Loudoun Co., Va., Guardian Accounts, A:16-17, 29 September 1772; County Clerk's Office, Leesburg. Cato's appearance as a defendant in (uncle?) James Winn's 1779 discontinued suit "on an attachment" supports his birth no later than 1758 to then have been age twenty-one; Fauquier Co., Va., Minute Book 1773-1780, 400, 27 July 1779; FHL microfilm 31,614. The date when Winn brought the suit is not known. St. George Tucker, *Blackstone's Commentaries with Notes of Reference* (1803), v.2, chapter 17, Of Guardian and Ward, "An infant cannot be sued but under the protection, and joining the name, of his guardian...infant, under twenty one"; online transcription (https://lonang.com/library/ reference/tucker-blackstone-notes-reference/).

[31] William Waller Hening, ed., "An Act for dividing the County of Fairfax," April 1757, in *The Statutes at Large: Being a Collection of all the Laws of Virginia from the First Session of the Legislature in the year 1619*, 13 vols. (Richmond, Va.: privately printed, 1820), 7:148.

[32] Loudoun Co., Va., Will Book A:73, will of William West Jr., 15 November 1762, proved 12 April 1763.

[33] Loudoun Co., Va., Will Book A:226, will of William West (Sr.), 26 June 1769, proved 13 November 1769; FHL microfilm 32, 275.

[34] Ibid.

[35] Loudoun Co., Va., Guardian Accounts, A:16-17, 29 September 1772; County Clerk's Office, Leesburg.

[36] Loudoun Co., Va., Chancery Case M2993 (West v. West, 1786-011), 14 June 1771.

[37] William West Sr.'s 1769 will identified four sons: the late William Jr. (father of Cato and Charles), John, Thomas, and Charles (Loudoun Co., Va., Will Book A:226). The will directed Thomas to provide annual payments to John,

Cato and Charles's mother Mary (Winn) West had remarried in 1765 to John Smith of adjacent Fauquier County, Va.,[38] and produced two more sons by September 1771.[39] Apparently after Cato West reached age twenty-one, James Winn (likely Cato's uncle) sued Cato West in 1779 "on an attachment" in Fauquier County; the suit was discontinued.[40]

South Carolina

By 1779, Cato West had long since followed at least one of his maternal Winn uncles to South Carolina where, at the beginning of the American Revolution, he joined residents of the Camden District[41] in signing a petition addressed to Robert Ellison on 2 September 1775 requesting permission to form a volunteer company of rangers.[42] Cato West served as a private in 1777 under his uncle Captain Richard Winn in the South Carolina Rangers,[43] which had been designated as the 3rd South Carolina Regiment in 1775 and adopted into the Continental Line on 24 July 1776.[44]

In Georgia, Capt. Winn's 52-member South Carolina Ranger company, supplemented by a 23-member detachment of the 1st Georgia Battalion, could not hold Fort McIntosh against the British and Indians' attack on 17 February 1777, and Winn's "surrendered prisoners of war" list

---

and John is not found in Loudoun County records after 1784 when he was last charged to brother Charles as a tithable (*FamilySearch* (www.familysearch.org), "List of Tithables, 1758-1799," Loudoun County, 1784, Peirce Bayly's list, image 871, Charles West, John West; FHL microfilm 31,052). No marriage or probate records have been found for John West of Loudoun County. Thomas left a will dated 1776 mentioning siblings, nieces, and nephews, but no children (Loudoun Co., Va., Will Book B:142). Charles left a will dated 1777 providing for his two minor daughters and for a £60 payment for "a boy about two years old which is a son from my servant Woman nam'd Thomas" when he reached age twenty (Loudoun Co., Va., Will Book C:58, will of Charles West, 29 January 1777, proved 8 January 1787; FHL microfilm 32,275). If, as it appears, this was Charles West's son, then this young Thomas may have been the "Thomas Dougherty a base born son of Mary Dougherty" whom the Cameron Parish Churchwardens bound to "Charles West, Gentleman," on 12 May 1778 (Loudoun Co., Va., Order Book G:94; FHL microfilm 32,349). If so, Thomas Dougherty's descendants might include males who continue the William West Sr.'s bloodline if not the West name.

[38] Loudoun Co., Va., Clerk's 1765 Fee Book, last page; Circuit Court Archives, Leesburg.

[39] Son John Smith chose Peter Grant as his guardian in 1784, showing he was at least fourteen at the time. See Fauquier Co., Va., Minute Book 1781–1784:283, April court 1784; FHL microfilm 31,614. Son Richard Smith chose (his uncle?) Minor Winn as his guardian in 1785. See Fauquier Co., Va., Minute Book 1784–1786:244, September Court 1785; FHL microfilm 31,615.

[40] Fauquier Co., Va., Minute Book 1773-1780:400, 27 July 1779, Winn v. West; FHL microfilm 31,614. The minute book does not list an earlier Winn v. West entry, so Winn's suit appears to have been brought and discontinued on the same court date. Fauquier County has surviving court records of this era, and this ended cause may be among them, but these "loose papers" are not indexed and are too fragile to be handled, according to guidance from its Records Room staff (2019 telephone conversation).

[41] Camden District in 1785 comprised what today includes the counties of Chester, Claremont, Clarendon, Fairfield, Lancaster, Richland, and York (https://www.familysearch.org /learn/wiki/en/Camden_District,_South_Carolina).

[42] "Papers of the First Council of Safety of the Revolutionary Party of South Carolina, June-November, 1775," *South Carolina Historical and Genealogical Magazine*, v.1 (July 1900), no.3, 195-196.

[43] "Copy, List of the Garrison of Fort McIntosh on St. Tilla River, surrendered Prisoners of War, this 18th February 1777," filed with "Lt. Col. Brown to Governor Tonyn, No.15 with 2 other Papers of the same Number," British Public Record Office, Colonial Office Records, Class 5, v.557, folios 177-178, pages 353-355; digital images from microfilm, University Archives and West Florida History Center, University of West Florida, Pensacola.

[44] Robert K. Wright, Jr., *The Continental Line* (Washington, D.C.: U.S. Army, Center of Military History, 1983), 307.

of 18 February 1777 includes Private "Cator" West but notes that he was one of five who were "absent."[45]

West was commissioned as a first lieutenant apparently in March 1777.[46] The original commissions "appear to no longer be extant."[47] South Carolina's colonial government would have approved Continental Line commissions but "[t]he body that could have approved [Continental Line] commissions, the House of Representatives, has not extant journals for the period October 1776-August 1779."[48]

Francis Marion's orderly book recorded "Gen[era]l. Orders by Genl. [Robert] How[e]" emanating from a Charleston court martial held on 21 September 1778: "Lt. Colo. [*sic*] West of 3rd Regt. having resigned his commission the 14th Inst. is no longer to be respected & obeyed a Continental officer."[49] As this information had been "transmitted" to Marion, the copyist entering it into the orderly book likely misread "Lt. *Cato* West" as "Lt. *Colo.* West."[50]

One bit of indirect, non-contemporary, and uncorroborated evidence asserts that West held the rank of captain at some point. According to notes made in 1855 by Col. R. M. Edwards of Bradley County, Tennessee, his neighbor, friend, or relative John Latta/Latty (b."1762?") lived and enlisted in Chester County, South Carolina, and served under "Capt. Cato West" in Col. Thomson's S.C. regiment. Latta did not specify when West was his captain and claimed his company never "gathered together" again after Sumpter's defeat on 18 August 1780.[51]

Western North Carolina—now Tennessee
Cato West migrated to the area of North Carolina that is now the northeastern corner of Tennessee, where in 1781 he acquired two enslaved boys, Jupiter and John, in separate

---

[45] "Copy, List of the Garrison of Fort McIntosh on St. Tilla River, surrendered Prisoners of War, this 18th February 1777." West is listed as the 24th private. The list also includes annotations of two others who were "wounded."
[46] Francis Bernard Heitman's *Historical Register of Officers of the Continental Army during the War of the Revolution, April 1775 to December 1783* (1892), 3. Heitman examined "the various military rolls, lists, orders, and other records of the Revolutionary War, on file in the various Executive Departments of the Government" (p.3) and lists Cato West as "1st Lieutenant 5th South Carolina—March, 1777; resigned—October 1778" (p.428); (https://archive.org/details/ historicalregist00heit/page/428). Heitman's source for West's 1777 commission (and the erroneous resignation date) remains unidentified.
[47] South Carolina Department of Archives and History (SCDAH), staff letter to author, 26 August 2019.
[48] SCDAH, staff letter to author, 5 September 2019.
[49] Francis Marion's Orderly Books, v.1, pt. 2: 2 May 1777 – 6 May1779, microfilm roll 2, f.3; James A. Rogers Library, Francis Marion University, Florence, S.C.; originals at Huntington Library, San Marino, Calif. Patrick O'Kelley, *Unwaried Patience and Fortitude: Francis Marion's Orderly Book* (West Conshohocken, Penn.: Infinity Publishing Co., 2006), 350. Resignations were common enough in 1778 to warrant mention by General Washington: Letter from George Washington to John Bannister, 21 April 1778, transcription, *Founders Online* (https://founders.archives.gov/documents/Washington/03-14-02-0525): "The spirit of resigning Commissions has long been at an alarming height and increases daily."
[50] O'Kelley, *Unwaried Patience and Fortitude*, fn 907 on p.673: "Lieutenant Cato West was only a lieutenant. He had served in an independent ranger company under Captain Robert Ellison in 1775. In March 1777 he became a lieutenant in the 3rd South Carolina (Ranger) Regiment. He resigned on 14 September 1778 after the failed Georgia expedition."
[51] *The Latta Genealogy Newsletter* (http://www.latta.org/Notes/Notes/Note%20W.htm), Our Database>View/ download the Branch Notes>Note W – John Latta or Latty.

transactions recorded in Washington County.[52] The following spring, he gave his residence as Sullivan County, adjoining Washington County, when giving his brother Charles West power of attorney to sell his land in Loudoun County, Va.[53]

Around 1780-1782, Cato West married Martha, a daughter of Thomas Green.[54] Green, West, and a multi-family expedition set out from the Holston River in Tennessee, reputedly for the available land of the Northwest Territory, but the difficult currents of the Ohio River forced them to change course and they headed for the lower Mississippi River instead.[55]

Natchez District, Spanish West Florida
A Spanish census taken 6 July 1782 recorded the 13 American families that arrived in Natchez in May 1782, including Cato West with his unnamed wife, son, and eight slaves, listed in sequence with his father- and brother-in-law's families:

Famillias	Individuos	Esclavos
1...Thomas Green, su Muger y hijos	11	32
1...Thomas Marston Green, Muger y hijo	3	11
1...Cato West, su Muger y hijo	3	8.[56]

Within a year, Cato West had acquired and sold a 20-foot-square house on a 39' by 102' lot adjoining his father-in-law's in Natchez.[57]

---

[52] Washington County, Tennessee, "Court of Pleas Minute Book 1, 1778-1801," 134, 28 May 1781, Thos. Hardiman acknowledges sale of "one negro fellow named Jupiter" to Cato West; FHL microfilm 825,510. Also, on page 142, on 27 August 1781, Hardiman acknowledges sale of "one negro Boy slave named Jupiter" (same male or a younger male of the same name?) to Cato West, and Michael Massengill acknowledges sale to Cato West of "a negro Boy named John about eight years of age." Later land records refer to property that Cato West owned near Cedar Creek in Washington County, for which a grant or deed of purchase has not been located (Washington Co., Tenn., Deed Book 3:100-101, 26 October 1786, North Carolina grant no. 752 to Isaac Lane, 76 acres, adjoining William Bean and Cato West; FHL microfilm 825,523).

[53] Loudoun Co., Va., Deed Book N:511, power of attorney from Cato West of Sullivan County, North Carolina, to "Brother Charles West" of Loudoun Co., Va., 11 March 1782, proved 13 April 1782 in Washington Co., N.C. by Robert Allison (his former captain?) and Zechariah Smith who also saw "Col. John Winn" witness the document; FHL microfilm 32,303.

[54] West had married Green's daughter before 1784. *FamilySearch* (www.familysearch.org), "Original Spanish Record, 1781-1796," Spanish Records vol. 4-5 1783-1784, vol. 5:305, image 536, original power of attorney by Thomas Green to "my loving sons, Thomas Marston Green, Cato West, and Abner Green," 6 June 1784; FHL microfilm 886,356. See also May Wilson McBee, compiler, *The Natchez Court Records, 1767-1805, Abstracts of Early Records* (Greenwood, Miss.: by the compiler, 1953), "Natchez Court Records, 1781-1798," page 135, abstract of the power of attorney; citing Court Records Book D, page 3.

[55] John Francis Hamtramck Claiborne, *Mississippi, as a Province, Territory, and State, with Biographical Notices of Eminent Citizens* (Jackson, Miss.: Power & Barksdale, 1880), 96, footnote. May Wilson McBee, *The Life and Times of David Smith; Patriot, Pioneer, and Indian Fighter* (Kansas City: Mendenhall, 1959), 23-24.

[56] "Relación de Las famillias Americanas que Llegaron a Ese Puerto [En?] el mes de Mayo del Corriente Año 1782" [American families who arrived in this port (Natchez) in May 1782], 6 July 1782; Archivos General de las Indias [AGI], Papeles Procedentes de la isla de Cuba [PPC], edición 106, legajo 193-b, handwritten folio no. 462; Archivo General de Indias, Seville, Spain; copy provided from PPC microfilm roll 29, The Historic New Orleans Collection, New Orleans.

[57] McBee, *Natchez*, 18, citing Court Record A:128, sold to William Barland for $100, recorded 8 March 1783.

On 6 June 1784, Thomas Green gave power of attorney to "my loving sons, Thomas Marston Green, Cato West, and Abner Green."[58] Virginia records document Cato West's father as William West Jr., so Thomas Green implied an in-law, rather than biological, relationship. Twenty years later, a deed shows Cato and wife "Patsey" West joining with her Green siblings, including Abner and Thomas Marston Green, thus confirming that Cato West's wife, in 1804 at least, was Thomas's daughter "Patsey" or Martha Green.[59] A non-contemporary transcribed Green family Bible identifies Martha Wills Green, born 25 December 1763, as the daughter of Thomas Green and Martha Wills, as the wife of Cato West, and as the mother of Cato's earliest documented children.[60]

However, early Daughters of the American Revolution (DAR) applications claim that Cato West married Martha's younger sister, Ann Howard Green. The Green family Bible identifies this sister as Ann "Harwood" Green, born 17 December 1765, without a husband listed. The DAR applications that depict Ann as Cato's wife show her as the mother of a Martha West, born 1810, who married a Montgomery[61] but evidence described later confirms this child Martha was born to Cato's later non-Green spouse. Cato West would be Thomas Green's son-in-law regardless of whether Cato married Martha or Ann Green, and the possibility of Ann Harwood Green as Cato's first wife has not be ruled out.

A 1784 Spanish census recorded two years after the Wests' arrival showed the addition of a female in Cato West's household, a reduction in the number of slaves (to four), and the ownership of 30 cattle, 10 horses, and 60 or 80 hogs.[62] By 1787, his household on Cole's Creek had two adult males, one young male, one adult female, and one young female. In addition to livestock, this census also noted that Cato West had 5,000 pounds of tobacco and 800 bushels of corn "in ears," and that his household had one firearm and two individuals "able to carry arms."[63]

The 1792 census—"Padron del Districto de Natchez"—enumerated Cato West's family of eight individuals and four slaves as residents of the Villa Gayoso district, which encompassed their land holdings on Cole's Creek.[64] Just before the United States established its own government there, businessman Manuel Garcia de Texada referred to Cato West as a settler and mayor of the

---

[58] McBee, *Natchez*, 135, citing Court Record D:3 for Thomas Green's 6 June 1784 power of attorney.

[59] Jefferson Co., Miss., Deed Book B1:44 (p.33 of the typed transcription), Cato and Patsey West et al. to Everard Green, 1 April 1804, recorded 25 February 1805; FHL microfilm 892,552.

[60] Bible Records of Colonel Thomas Marston Green, family pages only, transcription, p.13, "Children of Cato West and Martha Will[s] Green"; digital images 6372029–6372042 of supporting documentation for the NSDAR application of Ellen Frances (O'Leary) Bundschu (national no. 373,979) on Thomas Marston Green (1723-1805, South Carolina), approved January 1948; National Society, Daughters of the American Revolution (NSDAR), Washington, D.C.

[61] NSDAR applications of Lotta Moore Armistead (nat.no.117,606), Lottie Montgomery (nat.no.137,563), and Annie Montgomery Hall (nat.no.141298).

[62] [Census of the District of Natchez], 1784; Papeles Procedentes de la isla de Cuba, legajo 116, folio 519, sixteenth entry on page; Clayton Library, Houston.

[63] "Natchez 18 de Enero de 1787" [Census of the District of Natchez], 1787; Papeles Procedentes de la isla de Cuba, legajo 200, folio 596, last entry for Cole's Creek; Clayton Library, Houston: Cato West, males 2-2-0, females, 1-1-0, mulatto slaves: none; negro slave males 0-3-0, females 1-2-0; 30 cattle, 10 horses, 0 sheep, 60 hogs; 5,000 lbs. tobacco, 800 bushels of corn in ears, 12 individuals; 2 able to carry arms; 1 firearm. Age category headers missing.

[64] "Mississippi, State and Territorial Census Collection, 1792-1866," images, *Ancestry* (www.ancestry.com), 1792>Natchez>Villa Gayoso, image 2, Cato West; citing Heritage Quest microfilm V229.

Villa Gayoso district.[65] West and his cohorts obtained land through Spanish grants of their own or as purchased from others who had entered claims.[66] By 1800 Cato had obtained over 2,200 acres in three tracts on branches of Cole's Creek.[67] Two of these tracts he divided among three of his sons, but the third tract he retained until his death.[68] Meanwhile, Cato's brother, Dr. Charles West, and his family had also left Loudoun County, Virginia, and settled in the Natchez area about 1791.[69]

Mississippi Territory

The United States established a government in the newly acquired Mississippi Territory on 7 April 1798.[70] Mississippi territorial governor Winthrop Sargent in April 1799 established the counties of Adams (the location of Natchez) and Pickering (the location of Cato West's land).[71] By 11 January 1802, the Legislative Council and House of Representatives of the Mississippi Territory passed "An Act to alter the name of Pickering County" to Jefferson County.[72]

Governor Sargent commissioned Cato West as Pickering County militia's lieutenant-colonel commandant on 8 September 1798 but West resigned in 1799.[73] Historical publications document Cato West's political activities, especially with his father-in-law Thomas Green. President Thomas Jefferson recommended, and the U.S. Senate confirmed, Cato West as

---

[65] Jefferson Co., Miss., Deed Book A2:45, Manuel Garcia de Texada to Cato West, "havitanto y alcalde del districto Villa Gayoso," 7 March 1798; FHL microfilm 892,552.

[66] U.S. Congress, *American State Papers: Documents, Legislative and Executive of the Congress of the United States*, Walter Lowrie, ed. (Washington, D.C.: Duff Green, 1834), 1:776, Cato West, certificate A25 issued 19 April 1805. Original survey no. 33870, 30 June 1806, Cato West, certificate no. A25, 758.11 acres on Cole's Creek, Section 54, T9N R1W, Washington Meridian; photocopy, Mississippi Secretary of State's Office, Jackson, Miss. The BLM's August-November 2019 search did not locate a tract book entry or patent for this land. *American State Papers: Public Lands*, Duff Green ed., 1:776, certificate A27 issued 19 April 1805. Cato West claim, Mississippi, serial no. 013090, Serial Patent Files 1908-1951, RG 49; National Archives, Washington, D.C. (NA-Washington) [patent no. 1123194, 8 February 1948, Section 11, T9N, R1W and Section 45, T10N, R1W, Washington Meridian, 1,238.37 acres]. *American State Papers: Public Lands*, Duff Green ed., 1:813, certificate C9 issued 3 February 1807. Cato West claim, Mississippi, serial no. 010163, Serial Patent Files 1908-1951, RG 49; NA-Washington, D.C. [patent no. 1119300, 5 January 1945, Section 8, T9N, R1E, and Section 10N, R1E, Wash. Mer., 260 acres].

[67] See General Land Office original survey plats for Cato West's Sections no. 11 and 54 in T9N R1W; Section 8 in T9N R1E; Section 45 in T10N R1W, and Section 45 in T10N, R1E. Cato West's tracts overlap these township and range boundaries.

[68] Jefferson Co., Miss., Deed Book B1:280 (201 typed), Cato West conveyed for love, goodwill, and affection to son William West, 25 July 1808 (FHL microfilm 892,552); Deed Book C1:168; Cato West for affection to son Thomas West, 1 July 1815, recorded 28 August 1815 (includes plat); and Deed Book C1:169, Cato West for affection to son Charles West, 1 July 1815, recorded 28 August 1815, (includes plat); (FHL microfilm 892,553).

[69] See "4. Charles West" section.

[70] United States Congress, *The Public Statutes at Large* (Boston: Charles C. Little and James Brown, 1845), vol. 1:549, Fifth Congress, 2nd Session, Chapter 28, "An Act...authorizing the establishment of a government in the Mississippi territory."

[71] *The Statutes of the Mississippi Territory, Revised and Digested by the Authority of the General Assembly*, Hon. Harry Toulmin, comp. (Natchez: Samuel Terrell, Printer to the Mississippi Territory, 1807), 2-3: Part One, "III. Proclamation."

[72] Ibid., Part One, 3, "V. An act to alter the name of Pickering County."

[73] Dunbar Rowland, ed., *The Official and Statistical Register of the State of Mississippi, 1908* (Nashville, Tenn.: Brandon Printing Co., 1908), 15. Robert Haynes, *The Mississippi Territory and Southwest Frontier, 1795-1817* (Lexington, Ky.: University Press of Kentucky, 2010), 31.

Secretary of the Mississippi Territory in March 1803.[74] West also served as the acting territorial governor from 1 October 1804 to 10 May 1805, and as superintendent of Indian Affairs, during this period when temporary duty kept governor William C. C. Claiborne in Louisiana.[75]

A territorial census of Jefferson County in 1805 listed the families of Cato and of his eldest son William:

> Cato West, 4 males over 21, 6 males under 21, 6 females, 32 slaves
> William West, 1 male over 21, 1 male under 21, 1 female, 7 slaves.[76]

Evidence indicates that personal and professional factors weighed heavily upon West during this time. His family had grown to include eleven children and his 1805 household consisted of fourteen people.[77] His eldest and married daughter Martha (West) Davidson had died,[78] and his own wife Martha (Green) West followed shortly thereafter.[79] On July 8, 1805, Cato West wrote to U.S. Secretary of State James Madison, resigning his office as secretary.[80] A federal case brought after his death stated that, on 9 May 1806, Cato West became indebted to the United States in the amount of $406.53, for goods, wares, merchandise, work, care, diligence, money

---

[74] *Journal of the Executive Proceedings of the Senate of the United States of America, from the commencement of the First, to the termination of the Nineteenth Congress*, (Washington, D.C.: Duff Green, 1828), 446-447.

[75] Dunbar Rowland, Director, *An Official Guide to the Historical Materials in the Mississippi Department of Archives and History* (Nashville: Brandau-Craig-Dickerson Co., 1914), 51, "Territorial Archives (1789-1817), Series A, Governors' Records, Vol. 5, Administration of Acting-Governor Cato West, October 1, 1804-May 10, 1805." However, the sitting governor William C. C. Claiborne departed Mississippi on assignment in December 1803; "Mississippi History Timeline," Mississippi Department of Archives and History (https://www.mdah.ms.gov/timeline/?s=claiborne). Dunbar Rowland, Director, *Second Annual Report...Mississippi Department of Archives and History* (Nashville: Brandon Printing Company, 1904), 51.

[76] *FamilySearch* (www.familysearch.org), "Mississippi territorial census: RG 2, series 497, 1801-1816," Territorial census, Box 17981, Jefferson County, 1805, digital film 4822295, image 100, Cato West and William West; citing Mississippi Department of Archives and History (hereinafter MDAH), Jackson, Mississippi.

[77] Ibid.

[78] The remarriage of Martha's husband places her death before 19 May 1803. Jefferson Co., Miss., Deeds A2:77, Davidson-Green marriage, recorded 1 September 1803; FHL microfilm 892,552.

[79] Martha appears, as "wife Patsey," with husband Cato in a deed dated 1 April 1804 but did not sign (Jefferson Co., Miss., Deed Book B1:44 (p.33 of the typed transcription), Cato and Patsey West et al. to Everard Green, 1 April 1804, recorded 25 February 1805; FHL microfilm 892,552). The tombstone of her last child, Benjamin Franklin West, claims he was born 13 March 1805; *Find a Grave* (www.findagrave.com), Benjamin Franklin West, 22 August 1845, memorial 5636955, by William Sanders; photograph (Wintergreen Cemetery, Claiborne Co., Miss.). Martha was deceased before Cato's subsequent marriage in 1810.

[80] David W Parker, *Calendar of Papers in Washington [D.C.] Archives Relating to the Territories (to 1873)* (Washington, D.C.: Carnegie Institution of Washington, 1911), 216, Territorial Papers, Mississippi, no.4275: Bureau of Rolls and Library in the Department of State, "Claiborne cor[respondence].," volume 3.

lent, advanced, paid out and expended.[81] His daughter Elizabeth "Betsy" (West) Balch died on 25 January 1807,[82] and his first-born son William West died by the summer of 1810.[83]

The summer of 1810 also saw the remarriage of Cato, then about age fifty. Cato West married teenaged[84] Martha "Patsey" Harper, daughter of Jesse and Martha ([Jones?]) Harper,[85] on 12 August 1810 in Jefferson County, M.T.[86] Six months later, another of Cato's married daughters died: Mary, wife of Edward Turner.[87] Cato's new father-in-law Jesse Harper bequeathed three young slaves—Jenny, Nancy, and Hannah—to daughter Martha (Harper) West in his 9 August 1811 will, noting that none of his eight children yet had offspring.[88] In December 1812, Cato and Martha's first child, Martha Elizabeth, was born.[89] Their children Mary Louisa, Cato Jr., and William followed. Three of the four children born to this second marriage bear the same names as Cato's then-deceased children by his first wife: Martha, Mary, and William. The eldest child of this second marriage—Martha Elizabeth—would be the only one of the four to survive to adulthood and marry.

Cato West and his son-in-law Dr. Hezekiah J. Balch with two others represented Jefferson County at the convention in 1817 to adopt a constitution for the newly created state of Mississippi, formed from the western part of the Mississippi Territory, with Alabama being formed from the eastern part.[90] When the delegates finalized and adopted a draft of Mississippi's

---

[81] U.S. v. Cato West's Executors, January Term 1822-April Term 1824, "U.S. District Court, Natchez, Miss., Record Book, 1819-1824," 379-399, 1 January 1822; Records of the District Courts of the U.S., Record Group 21, National Archives, Southeastern Region, Atlanta, Ga. (NA-Atlanta). Defense attorney (and Cato's former son-in-law) Edward Turner claimed West repaid this debt on 1 January 1807 but Turner lost the case to his son-in-law, the prosecuting district attorney William B. Griffith (husband of Cato's granddaughter Theodosia Turner). See receipts for payments to the U.S. and for Turner's services in West's probate packet B-98).

[82] *Mississippi Messenger* (Natchez, M.T.), Tuesday, 27 January 1807, v.3, no.126, p.2, col.4.

[83] Jefferson Co., Miss., Chancery Court, probate packet A-79, W[illiam]. West, administrators' bond, 23 July 1810; FHL microfilm 1,888,885. Jefferson Co., Miss., Probate Records, A2, (page illegible), inventory of William West estate, 28 August 1810, recorded 30 January 1811; FHL microfilm 893,041.

[84] The eldest female in the 1830 U.S. census entry for Martha Harper's second husband William L. Davis's household is presumed to be Martha, then age 30-40 or born 1790-1800 (Jefferson Co., Miss., p. 27 stamped, 183 written, third entry from bottom of the page; NARA microfilm M19, roll 71). An undocumented genealogy indicates Martha Harper was age sixteen at marriage: Lynn Wood, *Donahoe Nexus* (Renton, Wash.: Nexus Publications, 1989-1996), Winter 1990, p.14: "born ca 1794 in Georgia."

[85] Jefferson Co., Miss., Probate Records A2:20, will of Jesse Harper, 9 August 1811, proved 28 October 1811; FHL microfilm 893,041. He mentions wife Martha and daughter Martha West. NSDAR application (national no. 711183) on Jesse Harper (1734-1811, Virginia) asserts wife's name as "Martha Jones" but without documentation; future DAR applicants must prove service and that Martha Jones is mother of Jesse's children.

[86] "Married," *Raleigh Register and North Carolina (State) Gazette*, 16 August 1810, v.11, no.569, p.3, col. 4: "In Jefferson County, M.T. on the 12th inst. Col. Cato West, to Miss Patsey Harper."

[87] "Sketch of the Life of the Hon. Edward Turner," *Reports of Cases Argued and Determined in the High Court of Errors and Appeals for the State of Mississippi* (Boston: Charles C. Little & James Brown, 1844), W. C. Smedes and T. A. Marshall, reporters to the state, 10-12.

[88] Jefferson Co., Miss., Probate Records A2:20, will of Jesse Harper, 9 August 1811, proved 28 October 1811).

[89] Ann Beckerson Brown, *Jefferson Co., Mississippi, Cemeteries, Etc.,* vol. 2 (Shreveport, La.: J & W Enterprises, 1996), 99. Birth date calculated from her age at death as inscribed on her tombstone, according to this published transcription.

[90] "Mississippi Territory, Delegates to the Convention," *Carthage Gazette* (Carthage, Tenn.), 1 July 1817, v.8, issue 31, p.3, col.4.

first constitution, only West "refused thus to give his sanction to the dismemberment of the territory."[91]

Illness apparently visited Cato West's family severely enough in 1818 that he and his eldest surviving son, Thomas, drafted their wills and both also named Charles West—Cato's son and Thomas's brother—to serve as executor.[92] On 30 July 1818, Cato signed his will at his "Fairfield" homeplace:[93]

> I Cato West of Jefferson County in the State of Mississippi do make, ordain, and declare the following my last Will and Testament. I give and bequeath to my wife Martha West to her and her heirs forever in lieu of her dower in my personal estate my negroes Marmada & Henry and all her children, Banda [?], Binna [?] and her child William, Nancy and her child Anna and her [son Jr.?] , and the girl Sally Bought of Morgan and Sikes [?], and all of the negroes I am entitled to from her father's estate by her -- one halfe my household furniture of every kind, all my kitchen utensils, one of my best saddle horses that she may prefer, one Third of my Teames, carts, and plantation tools, and one third of my stock of Cattle, sheep, and hogs. My other children having been provided for as I deemed suitable, and agreeable to my circumstances; I give and bequeath to my six youngest Children, namely John Smith, Richard Claiborne, Benjamin Franklin, Martha Elizabeth, Mary Louisa, and Cato West and also the one my wife is now pregnant with to them and their heirs forever, all the residue of my estate both real and personal to be equally divided amongst them as may be without [soi? sale?] but of surplus produce, and out lying stockes not only commanded except as is herein after provided, each child's part to be delivered as follows, that is to say, to my sons at the age of twenty one years and my Daughters at the same age, or sooner if they should marry Provided nevertheless that my son Cato shall not be entitled to any of my lands, except that part on which I now reside that lies on the [east?] side of the Creek, together with all the several tracts and parcels adjoining it on the same side of the Creek to Include the lands purchased of Wm Stampley also, all of which lands I give and bequeath to him and his heirs forever reserving however to my wife, in lieu of her dower in my lands my residence in the mansion house and the use of so much of the premises as may be necessary for her purposes during life and provided further that there shall be and I do hereby reserve two acres to include the present burying ground as a burying place in common for my family and others forever:-- I also give to my said son Cato my two desks sideboard, clock, watch, and all my books, to be delivered to him whenever my wife shall think proper. It is my desire that the estate herein bequeathed to my children, shall be kept together, and delivered out to them as is provided above, according to the [??] there may be in the mass at the several periods when a child's part [shall?] be delivered into his or her possession. -- And now for the due execution of this my last will and testament I do hereby nominate and appoint my beloved wife Martha West executrix, and my worth[y ??] Cowles Mead Esquire, and my son Charles West executors confiding in them to do all things necessary and proper for a due execution thereof. In Testimony whereof I have hereunto signed my name and affixed my seal at Fairfield the place of my residence the thirtieth day of July in the year of our Lord one

---

[91] *Proceedings of the…annual meeting of the Mississippi State Bar Association* (Jackson, Miss.: Hederman Bros., 1910), v.10, 109-110.

[92] Jefferson Co., Miss., Will Book A:24-25, consecutively recorded wills of Thomas West, (written 18 August 1818) and Cato West (written 30 July 1818); proved or recorded dates not in will book; FHL microfilm 893,068. The identical will book was filmed again in 1994 as FHL microfilm 1,939,756.

[93] "Fairfield" denotes Cato's Section 54, T9N, R1W, as demonstrated by his description (1) of "Fairfield" as his residence and (2) of "several tracts and parcels adjoining it…to Include the lands purchased of Wm. Stampley," the latter of whom patented Section 56, T9N, R1W (patent no. 1119294) and sold it to West (Jefferson Co., Miss., Deed Book C-1:167-168, Stampley to West, 28 August 1815; FHL microfilm 892,553).

thousand eight hundred and eighteen. --
In presence of   Cato West {seal}
Isaac McClutche
Robert Cocks
Adam Cloud[94]

Cato West's will was proved on 22 February 1819,[95] but estate records provide some clues to the actual date of Cato West's death in early 1819. Dr. Bullen's bill for services rendered showed almost daily visits to "self" (Cato) between 20 and 28 December 1818, remaining "all night" on that last date:

Decr 20	visit to self, medicine & prescript	7.00
22	visit to self	5.00
23	visit & prescript	6.00
25	visit & prescript	6.00
25	visit & advice for self	5.00
	medicine for negro woman	2.00
27	visit & advice	6.00
28	visit to self Detention all	
	night & attend	15.00
1819		
Jany 1	visit to self	4.00
Febr 7	ʒi Laudanum	1.00[96]

Bullen's final visit to "self" is dated 1 January 1819, after which the next charge is for laudanum for an unspecified household member on 7 February 1819.[97] Henry Siebe's bill for making a coffin for "Col. West" listed only that order's year, 1819, and that he had received payment therefor on 13 April 1819.[98]

There is another record, beyond these few estate receipts, that supports the deduction that Cato West died on 1 January 1819, and that his last child William was born on 7 February 1819. The probate packet for Cato's second father-in-law, Jesse Harper (d.1811), inexplicably includes a document pertaining to Cato's estate: "The Estate of Colo. Cato West Dec'd, in a/c to Wm. L. Davis for board."[99] William Davis married Cato West's widow in May 1820.[100] In his account

---

[94] Jefferson Co., Miss., Will Book A:24-25, will of Cato West, 30 July 1818.
[95] Jefferson Co., Miss., "Orphan [sic] Court Minutes 1814-1822," 108, Cato West's will was proved by two of the subscribing witnesses, Adam Cloud and Robert Cocks, and recorded at a special Orphans Court held on 22 February 1819; FHL microfilm 1,939,843. The previous court session was held on 24 January 1819.
[96] Jefferson Co., Miss., Chancery Court, probate packet B-98, estate of Cato West, bill from Dr. B[enjamin]. M[orse]. Bullen; FHL microfilm 1,889,020. The "ʒi" (or "Ezh") symbol in the medication entry denotes "one dram" of laudanum administered, per "Apothercaries' symbols commonly found in medical recipes" (www.textcreationpartnership.org/docs/dox/medical.html) and "Reading Old Prescriptions" (http://pharmacist/hubpages.com/hub/READING-OLD-PRESCRIPTIONS).
[97] Ibid. Perhaps administered to Mrs. West at birth of son William.
[98] Jefferson Co., Miss., Chancery Court, probate packet B-98, Cato West Jr.; FHL microfilm 1,889,020. Henry Siebe receipt.
[99] Jefferson Co., Miss., Chancery Court, probate packet A-93, Jesse Harper; FHL microfilm 1,888,885.
[100] *The Mississippi State Gazette* (Natchez, Miss.), 3 June 1820, v.8, no.23, p.2, col.3: "Married on the 30th ult. by the Reverend William Montgomery, Mr. Wm. L. Davis, to Mrs. Martha West, relict of the late Col. West; all of

worksheet, found in Harper's probate packet, Davis listed his costs for boarding three of Cato's children by first wife Martha Green and all four of Cato's children by Martha Harper (Davis's then-wife); the entries for the two youngest children reads:

> Cato West Jun'r Dec'd, one year & ten months
> from his father's death to his[;] 4 years old.
> William West Dec'd an infant three years old
> when he died[;] born after his father's Death.[101]

These minor heirs have separate probate packets. Cato West Jr.'s probate includes receipts that place his death between 13 and 15 November 1820.[102] "One year and ten months" prior to that would place Cato West Sr.'s death around 13-15 January 1819. This range falls within two weeks of the estimated date based on the doctor's last visit. Davis's entry for William West's boarding confirms that William was Cato's posthumous child but is less supportive of Cato West's death date as 1 January 1819 for the following reasons. Davis's entry described William West as three years old at his death, which occurred before 3 December 1821 according to William's own probate receipts.[103] If William were fully three years old at death, then that would place his birth, and his father Cato's death, prior to 3 December 1818. Cato West Sr. was attended by his doctor for the last time on 1 January 1819, so Davis's estimate of William West's age at death was likely slightly generous.

Despite Cato West's high political profile and lengthy residence in the area, no newspaper notice of his death has been located in surviving original or microfilmed newspapers of Natchez,[104] including the *Mississippi Republican* to which he subscribed.[105] Neither did a search of other indexed, digitized American newspapers uncover a notice picked up and published by newspapers in or beyond Mississippi.[106] The location of the ancient family cemetery has been

---

Jefferson county." Jefferson Co., Miss., Marriage Licenses and Certificates, A:154: William L. Davis and Mrs. Martha West, 30 May 1820 (year looks like 1821); FHL microfilm 893,070. After the death of husband William Davis, Martha (Harper) West Davis married 1837-1840 Robert Webb (d.bef.1852), who administered Davis's estate (with William Donoho serving as guardian of the Davis minors); Jefferson Co., Miss., Chancery Court, probate packets C:266, estate of William Davis (Jefferson Co., Miss., Chancery Court, probate packet C-266; FHL microfilm 1,901,943), and C:442, guardianship of Davis minors (FHL microfilm 1,902,402); Jefferson Co., Miss., Probate Records, E:189, Donoho seeks guardianship of minor Robert Webb, 1 March 1852; FHL microfilm 893,043. 1860 U.S. census, Arkansas Co., Ark., Arkansas twp., p.81 (stamped), dwelling 611, family 576, Martha (60, Miss.) and Robert L. (20, Miss.) Webb; NARA microfilm M653, roll 37. The 1861 tax list recorded "R. L. Webb (Estate)" as owning "NE4NE4, N2NW, NW4NE4," Section 34, T6S, R4W, 160 acres, $480, 7 slaves, $3,500, 2 cattle, 1 horse, tax $6.83 2/6; FHL microfilm 978,538.

[101] Jefferson Co., Miss., Chancery Court, probate packet A-93, Jesse Harper; FHL microfilm 1,888,885.

[102] Jefferson Co., Miss., Chancery Court, probate packet B-98, Cato West Jr.; FHL microfilm 1,889,020. One receipt is for a doctor's visit on the 13th and the other receipt is for a coffin ordered on the 15th.

[103] Jefferson Co., Miss., Chancery Court, probate packet B-93, William H. West; FHL microfilm 1,889,020.

[104] *Mississippi State Gazette* (Natchez, Miss.), v.7, published Wednesdays and Saturdays; "Mississippi 19th and 20th Newspapers in Original Format," Library of Congress control no. 8568. No death notice found in a search of the available issues (2, 6, 9, 16, 23, 27 January; 13, 20, 24 February, 3, 10, 13, 17, 24, 31 March 1819). A letter remaining at the Natchez post office for Cato West since 1 January 1819, advertised on 2, 6, and 9 January, was still not picked up by 9 January 1819 (v.7, no.3, p.4, col.3).

[105] Jefferson Co., Miss., Chancery Court, probate packet B-98, Cato West Jr. [*sic*]; FHL microfilm 1,889,020. Subscription receipt.

[106] NewsBank's "America's Historical Newspapers," *Ancestry's* "Newspapers.com," "NewspaperArchive," and Library of Congress's "ChroniclingAmerica."

tentatively identified on private property on the Natchez Trace but neither of the two surviving stones marks Cato West's final resting place.[107]

The children of Cato[3] West and Martha Wills Green:

5.   i.   WILLIAM[4] WEST, born possibly in Washington or Sullivan Co., N.C. (now Tenn.) by 1782; died in Jefferson Co., M.T., by the summer of 1810. He married Sarah Kirkland before 1805.

6.   ii. MARTHA ELIZABETH WEST, born in Mississippi Territory about 1782-1784; died about 1804. She married John A. Davidson on 6 May 1800 at Cole's Creek, Pickering (later Jefferson) Co., M.T.

7.   iii. MARY WEST, born in M.T. 1784-86; died in Claiborne Co., M.T., in 1811. She married Edward Turner before 4 November 1802 in Natchez, Adams Co., M.T.

8.   iv. THOMAS WEST, born in M.T. by 1787; died in Jefferson Co., Miss., in 1818.

9.   v.   ELIZABETH "BETSY" WEST, born in M.T. about 1789; died in Jefferson Co., M.T., on 25 January 1807. She married Dr. Hezekiah J. Balch on or after 5 January 1806 in Jefferson Co., M.T.

10. vi. CHARLES WEST, born in M.T. about 1791; died in Jefferson Co., Miss., on 22 October 1861. He married Charlotte E. Neely on 6 June 1820 in Jefferson Co., Miss.

11. vii. SUSAN WEST, born in M.T. by 1792; died in Jefferson Co., M.T., by 1816. She married her first cousin Thomas W. West before 1815.

12. viii. ANN WEST, born in M.T. about 1794; died in Holmes Co., Miss., on 5 September 1849. She married (1) Joseph Winn about 1811; (2) Elias F. Deloach 1834-1836 in Holmes Co., Miss.

13. ix. JOHN SMITH WEST, born in M.T. after 1797; died after attending one year, 1818-1819, of medical college in Philadelphia, Pa.

14. x.   RICHARD CLAIBORNE WEST, born in M.T. by 1804; died in Calhoun Co., Texas, in April 1847. He married Amelia Trahern by 1833, probably in Holmes Co., Miss.

15. xi. BENJAMIN FRANKLIN WEST, born in M.T. on 13 March 1805; died in Claiborne Co., Miss., on 22 August 1845. He married (1) Permelia, Pamela, or Paulina Meng(e) on 16 April 1829 in Jefferson Co., Miss., (2) Gabriella Johnston on 24 May 1826 in Jefferson Co., Ky.

The children of Cato West and Martha Harper:

16. i.   MARTHA ELIZABETH WEST, born in Jefferson Co., M.T. in December 1812; died in Jefferson Co. Miss., on 27 May 1845. She married James Jefferson Montgomery in Jefferson Co., Miss., on 11 March 1829.

---

[107] Brown, *Jefferson Co., Mississippi, Cemeteries, Etc.*, II:132: Susan Davis, died at the age of 5 years, 13 July 1834; Margaret C. Davis, died at the age of 4 months and 25 days, 5 July 1836. These stones appear to identify two Davis daughters born to Cato's second wife by the second of her three husbands. Their other children include Frances Dade Davis (who married William Donoho), Mary Jane Davis, Fenton H. Davis, and William L. Davis Jr. (Jefferson Co., Miss., Chancery Court, probate packets C-442, C-443, "C-442-443," and C-444; FHL microfilm 1,902,402).

17. ii. MARY LOUISA WEST, born in Jefferson Co., M.T., about 1814; died in Jefferson Co., Miss., in January 1833.
18. iii. CATO WEST, JR., born in Jefferson Co., M.T. about 1816; died in Jefferson Co., Miss., in November 1820.
19. iv. WILLIAM H. WEST, born in Jefferson Co., Miss., probably in February 1819; died in Jefferson Co., Miss., before 3 December 1821.

Dr. Charles West, full brother of Cato West

4. CHARLES[3] WEST (*William[2, 1]*), son of William West Jr. and Mary Winn, was born between 1751 and 1761 in Fairfax or Loudoun County, Virginia.[108] After his widowed mother married John Smith of Fauquier County, Charles likely grew up there, where he secured a marriage bond, on 10 June 1785, with Benjamin Withers security, to wed SARAH "SALLEY" WITHERS, whose father Thomas Withers gave written consent.[109] At some point Charles studied to become a doctor.

After the birth of sons Thomas W. and Cato Charles, Dr. West's family followed Cato to the Natchez District, likely where daughter Mary was born.[110] The obituary of one of Dr. West's sons placed that migration as occurring in 1791, noting also that Charles "was the first practicing physician in the Natchez District."[111] Charles, however, succumbed to an illness after making his will on 1 September 1795; the Spanish records of Natchez include both English and Spanish versions of it.[112] His will provided for his wife Sarah (Withers) West and children Thomas, Cato, and Mary. Charles named Sarah as executrix and included his "brother Cato West" as one of three appraisers:

> In the Name of God Amen I Charles West of the Dist. of Natchez being at present in a low state of health but of sound mind and memory I am movd [*sic*] to dispose of my worldly goods in manner hereafter directed but first of all recommending my spirit to him who gave it —

---

[108] Charles is identified as under age eighteen in his grandfather William's 26 June 1769 will, so he was born in or after 1751 (Loudoun Co., Va., Will Book A:226, will of William West (Sr.), 26 June 1769, proved 13 November 1769). Charles was given power of attorney by his brother Cato on 11 March 1782; if twenty-one, then born before 11 March 1761 (Loudoun Co., Va., Deed Book N:511, Cato West of Sullivan Co., N.C. to "Brother Charles West," 11 March 1782; FHL microfilm 32,303).

[109] Fauquier Co., Va., "Marriage Bonds and Returns, No. 1, 1759-1800," 143, Charles West and "Sally" Withers, 10 June 1785, typed 1933 transcript of bond and father's consent for "Salley" but no return; FHL microfilm 31,633.

[110] *The Weekly Standard* (Port Gibson, Miss.), 24 February 1866, v.1, no.16, p.1, col.4; quoting from *The Woodville Republican* (Woodville, Miss.), 27 January 1866, obituary of the late "Charles Cato West" of Wilkinson County: "His father, Dr. Charles West, removed to Mississippi Territory in 1791 and was the first practicing physician in the Natchez District. In company with him [*sic*] came his brother, Mr. Cato West." However, Charles West does not appear in the 1792 census of Natchez, Villa Gayoso.

[111] *The Weekly Standard* (Port Gibson, Miss.), 24 February 1866, obituary of Charles Cato West.

[112] *FamilySearch* (www.familysearch.org), "Original Spanish Record, 1781-1796," Spanish Records vol. 31-32 1795, vol. 32:322-335, images 539-542, original "testimento de Dr. Carlos West" (Spanish and English versions of Charles West's will and testimony proving it, with original signatures), 1 September 1795, proved 17 September 1795; FHL microfilm 893,509. *FamilySearch* catalogues these records under Adams County, Mississippi. The Spanish original and English translations of Dr. Carlos West's will identify his wife Sarah, children Thomas, Cato, and Mary, and "brother Cato West."

Item: I give and bequeath to my dear wife Sarah West my whole estate during her natural life or Widowhood but should either take place then in that case I desire that my estate be divided between my three children Thomas West Cato West & Mary West or as many of them as may be then living.

For the execution of this my last will and Testament I do hereby appoint my Dear & Loving wife my true lawful executrix Messrs. James Truly, David Odom & my Brother Cato West appraisers & that this my will be executed without the interference of [??].

In witness whereof I hereunto set my hand & affixed my se[al] [page 325] at the Dist. aforesaid this first day of September anno domini 1795.

Signd & seal'd in the Presence of us & each of us in the presence of the other

James Truly   Charles West [paper seal]
David Odom
Betsy Chaney
Everard Green
Parker Carradine
James E. Winn[113]

The widowed Sarah (Withers) West then married William Lemon; her sons confirmed that she died in Adams County, Mississippi, in 1822, and that her second husband died intestate in Mississippi in 1825.[114]

The children of Charles West and Sarah Withers:

i.   THOMAS W.[4] WEST, born about 1787 in Va.[115]; married (1) his first cousin Susan West perhaps about 1810; one child, *(a)* Martha Octavia.[116] Thomas married (2) Mary S. Chinn on 3 February 1818 in Wilkinson County, Miss.[117] Children by

---

[113] Ibid., original "testimento de Dr. Carlos West."

[114] West Feliciana Parish, Louisiana, Probate Records, Book 3 (not 4):359, petition filed 8 November 1826 by Cato C. and Thomas W. West against John Austin, curator of the estate of Wm. Lemon, both residents of Wilkinson Co.; FHL microfilm 364,676. "That the said William and Sarah lived together in wedlock untill sometime in A.D. 1822, when the said Sarah died in the county of Adams in the state aforesaid.... That sometime in A.D. 1825 the said William [Lemon] died without a will in the state of Mississippi...."

[115] Thomas's birth year estimate is based on the 1785 marriage of his parents, his mention as first among Charles's three children in the latter's will, and the 1789 birth year of his (presumed younger) brother Charles Cato West given in the latter's 1866 obituary. There is a solitary "Thomas West" in the 1808 territorial census of Jefferson County, but, lacking the "W." middle initial, it might pertain to his first cousin of the same name: *FamilySearch* (www.familysearch.org), "Mississippi territorial census: RG 2, series 497, 1801-1816," digital images, Territorial census, Box 17981, Jefferson County, 1808, digital film 4822295, p.3, image 110, Thomas West, over twenty-one.

[116] See "11. Susan West" section.

[117] Wilkinson Co., Miss., White Marriages (A-B, 1804-1823) A:28 bond; B:103-104 return, West-Chinn, 3 February 1818; FHL microfilm 877,597.

second wife:[118] *(b)* William T., b.1825-1830*[119]*; *(c)* John Connell, 1829-1832[120]; *(e)* Agatha M., b. January 1830[121]; *(f)* Margaret C., b.1830-1834.[122] Thomas died before 2 June 1833, on which date the announcement of his daughter Martha Octavia West's first marriage, to Lewis H. Davis, referred to him as the late Thomas W. West.[123]

ii.   CATO CHARLES WEST, born 3 August 1789 in Fauquier Co., Va.[124]; married Janet

---

[118] Thomas W. West's household included additional minors whose 1820, 1825, and 1830 census age ranges overlap, making it difficult to determine the total number of the couple's children. *Ancestry* (www.ancestry.com), "Mississippi, State and Territorial Census Collection, 1792-1866," database online (citing Heritage Quest microfilm v299); 1820, Wilkinson County, Miss., image 24, Thomas W. West ninth name, 1 male over twenty-one, 1 male under twenty-one, 1 female over twenty-one, [torn] female under twenty-one (followed by brother Cato C. West's entry); 1825, Wilkinson County, image 19, Thos. W. West: 0 white taxable, 0 slaves, 2 white males, 1 white female, 1 birth. 1830 U.S. census, Wilkinson Co., Miss., p. 274, Thos. W. West; NARA microfilm M19, roll 71.

[119] 1850 U.S. census, West Feliciana Par., La., p. 36 and 544 written, follows stamped p. 272B, dwelling 337, family 342, Mary West household with Wm. T., age twenty-six [Octavia (West) Malloy dwelling 335, family 340]; NARA microfilm M432, roll 231. 1860 U.S. census, West Feliciana Par., La., p.40 written, dwelling 339, family 342, M. J. West household with W.T. West, age thirty-four; NARA microfilm M653, roll 411.

[120] *Southern Planter* (Woodville, Miss.), 1 September 1832, v.1, no.35, p.3, col.2. "Obituary - Died, on Wednesday, 29th Ult., John Connell, son of Thomas W. West; aged 3 years."

[121] 1850 U.S. census, West Feliciana Par., La., p. 36 and 544 written, follows stamped p. 272B, dwelling 337, family 342, Mary West household with Agatha M., age nineteen; NARA microfilm M432, roll 231. 1860 U.S. census, West Feliciana Par., La., p.40 written, dwelling 339, family 342, M. J. West household with A. M. West, age twenty-six; NARA microfilm M653, roll 411. 1900 U.S. census, West Feliciana Par., La., 5th Ward, ED111, p.9A, dwelling and family 153, Agatha West household, born January 1830; NARA microfilm T623, roll 586.

[122] 1850 U.S. census, West Feliciana Par., La., pp. 36 and 544 written, follows stamped p. 272B, dwelling 337, family 342, Mary West household with Margaret C., age seventeen; NARA microfilm M432, roll 231. 1860 U.S. census, West Feliciana Par., La., p.40 written, dwelling 339, family 342, M. J. West household with M.C. West, age twenty-one; NARA microfilm M653, roll 411. 1900 U.S. census, West Feliciana Par., La., 5th Ward, ED111, p.9A, dwelling and family 153, Agatha West household with Margaret West, born February 1834; NARA microfilm T623, roll 586.

[123] Betty Couch Wiltshire, *Marriages and Deaths from Mississippi Newspapers*, vol. 3: 1813-1850 (Bowie, Md.: Heritage Books Inc., 1989), 220, citing the *Woodville Republican*, 8 June 1833: "dau of the late Thomas W. West, all of this county."

[124] "Death of a Veteran of 1814-15," *The Daily Picayune* (New Orleans), 31 January 1866, v.30, no.6, p.5, col.1; quoting from *The Woodville Republican* (Woodville, Miss.), 27 January 1866, "obituary of the late "Chas. Cato West, of Wilkinson county": "The deceased was born of an ancient English family, in Fauquier county, Va., on the 3rd day of August, A.D. 1789."

Scott Chinn on 2 September 1810 in Harrison Co., Ky.[125] Children: *(a)* perhaps Thomas Chinn[126] ; *(b)* perhaps William Howard[127] ; *(c)* Mary Agatha[128]; *(d)* Douglas[129]; *(e)* Walter[130]; *(f)* Sara Jane[131]; *(g)* Susan C.[132] Served in the War of 1812.[133] Died 6 January 1866 while on a visit to New Orleans, La.[134]

    iii.   MARY WEST, born about 1793,[135] probably in M.T.[136]; married Hezekiah J. Balch on 10 January 1808 in Adams Co., Miss.[137] Died 7 May 1816 in Greenville,

---

[125] Harrison County, Kentucky, Marriage Bond no. 693, West-Chinn, signed 28 August 1810 by Cato C. West and Chichester Chinn; FHL microfilm 216,879. Harrison Co., Ky., Marriage Returns, West-Chinn, 2 September 1810, return no. 641, which has multiple marriages performed by John Conner; FHL microfilm 216,891.

[126] Thomas C. West married Eliza "Cannell"/Connell on 6 March 1834 in Wilkinson Co., Miss. (*FamilySearch* (www.familysearch.org), "Mississippi Marriages, 1800-1911," database, Thomas C. West and Eliza Cannell, 6 March 1834; citing FHL microfilm 877,599). *New Orleans Weekly Delta* (New Orleans, La.), 7 August 1848, v.3, no.43, p.6, col.4: "Governor Johnson offers a reward of four hundred dollars for the arrest and conviction of Henry W. Barnes, who committed the crime of murder on the person of Thomas C. West, late of the parish of Pointe Coupee [La.]." Identical notice appears in the *Southern Sentinel* (Plaquemine, La.), 10 August 1848. 1850 U.S. census, Wilkinson Co., Miss., p.294-B, dwelling 405, family 409, Eliza West (age 32, born Miss.) with apparent children Richard (15, Miss.); Louis (10, Miss.); W.C. (8, Miss.); and Thos. C. (4, La.); NARA microfilm M432, roll 382.. No West family remained in Pointe Coupee Parish by 1850; the youngest child, Thomas C., was born about 1846 in Louisiana and apparently named after his father; the widow took her family back to Wilkinson County, Miss., after her husband's murder.

[127] *FamilySearch* (www.familysearch.org), "Mississippi Marriages, 1800-1911," database, William Howard West and Sarah Olivia Dunbar, 01 December 1837, Adams Co., Miss.; citing FHL microfilm 893,524. *Find a Grave* (www.findagrave.com), W. Howard West, 1815-16 August 1842, memorial 95324473 by Neville Wilson (Old Woodville Cemetery, Wilkinson Co., Miss.). *FamilySearch* (www.familysearch.org), "Mississippi Marriages, 1800-1911," database, Thomas B. Magruder and Sarah O. West, 16 April 1845; citing FHL microfilm 893,524. 1850 U.S. census, Jefferson Co., Miss., Twp. 9 East, p.102 stamped (203 written), dwelling and family 218, household of Thos. B. Magruder: Sarah O. Magruder (age 30, born Miss.), Wm. H. West (8, Miss.); NARA microfilm M432, roll 374.

[128] "Mrs. Mary A. Norwood," *Daily Picayune* (New Orleans), 16 September 1898, v.42, no.235, p.12, col.5.

[129] "Colonel Douglas West," *Daily Picayune* (New Orleans), 25 December 1901, v.45, no.335, p.9, col.7.

[130] 1850 U.S. census, Wilkinson Co., Miss., follows p.286B (stamped) and 572 (written), dwelling 272, family 276, C. C. West household; NARA microfilm M432, roll 382. Includes Walter among other Wests who are C. C. West's children per other sources.

[131] "Died," *Daily Picayune* (New Orleans), 12 November 1873, v.37, no.288, p.4, col.4; "Sara J. Murdock... daughter of the late C. C. West of Woodville, Miss."

[132] "Died," *Daily Picayune* (New Orleans), 15 March 1914, v.78, no.50, p.8, col.3; "Susan C. West, widow of the late McWilliam Wright." Identified as a sister in the obituaries of siblings Mary, Douglas, and Sara.

[133] Janet Scott West, widow's original pension application 9471 (Rejected), for service of Cato Charles West (Lt., Col. Robert Young's Detachment; Capt. Chance's Louisiana Militia, 1815), "War of 1812 Pension and Bounty Land Warrant Application Files," Record Group 15, NA-Washington. The application failed because West served fewer than the required 60 days. His son Douglas cited two War of 1812 bounty land warrants issued to his father: no. 100,380, 40 acres, 7 July 1854, and no. 74,230, 120 acres, issued 26 May 1856.

[134] *Weekly Standard* (Port Gibson, Miss.), 24 February 1866, v.1, no.6, p.1, col.4, reprinted obituary: "Death of a Veteran of 1814 and 1815; The Woodville Republican of the 27th ult., contains an obituary of the late "Charles Cato West" of Wilkinson county, who died in New Orleans while on a visit to that city, January 9th, 1866...."

[135] *Washington Republican and Natchez Intelligencer* (Natchez), Wednesday, 15 May 1816, v.4, no.4, p.3, col.3: "Died in the neighborhood of Greenville in Jefferson County on Tuesday evening, the 7th inst., Mrs. Mary Balch after a long and painful illness. She was in the 24th year of her age."

[136] Her brother's 1866 obituary stated that the family migrated to the Mississippi Territory in 1791.

[137] Adams Co., Miss., Marriages 1802-1819, vol. 1:51-52, Hezekiah J. Balch and Maria West, 4 January 1808; FHL microfilm 893,521. Her guardian (and stepfather) William Lemon consents.

Jefferson Co., Miss., leaving no children.[138] Hezekiah had first married Mary's first cousin, Elizabeth "Betsy" West.[139]

Children of Cato West and Martha Wills Green

5. WILLIAM[4] WEST (*Cato[3], William[2,1]*), son of Cato West and Martha Wills Green,[140] was born by 1782[141] likely in Washington or Sullivan Counties, North Carolina (later Tennessee), before his parents arrived in the Natchez District in May 1782 with him as their apparent only son.[142] He married SARAH KIRKLAND, daughter of Zachariah Kirkland and Martha Maria Raiford,[143] in 1803, according to her obituary.[144] On 5 August 1803, William recorded his cattle brand, and 11 days later his father Cato West recorded his.[145]

By 1805, the territorial census of Jefferson County recorded one male under age twenty-one in William and Sarah's household.[146] The household included another young white male by 1808,[147] in which year Cato West conveyed to his son William West a tract of 264 arpents on

---

[138] *Washington Republican and Natchez Intelligencer* (Natchez), 15 May 1816, Mrs. Mary Balch.

[139] Jefferson Co., Miss., Marriage Licenses and Certificates, A:17, Hezekiah J. Balch and Betsy West (license only), 5 January 1806; FHL microfilm 893,070.

[140] Jefferson Co., Miss., Deed Book B1:280, Cato West to "his son, William West," 25 July 1808; FHL microfilm 892,552.

[141] William was age twenty-one or older in 1805, and thus born before 1784. The 1784 Natchez census listed only one non-adult male in Cato West's household. Therefore, William appears to be the single male child of Cato West and wife recorded in July 1782 in Natchez. "Americanas...," 1782, Papeles Procedentes de la isla de Cuba [PPC], edición 106, legajo 193-b, handwritten folio no. 462; The Historic New Orleans Collection. [Census of the District of Natchez], 1784; PPC, legajo 116, folio 519; Clayton Library, Houston; Mississippi territorial census, Jefferson County, 1805; MDAH.

[142] William's father Cato West bought a slave in 1781 in Washington County, and recorded a power of attorney in 1782 in adjacent Sullivan County. Washington Co., Tenn., "Court of Pleas Minute Book 1, 1778-1801," 134, 28 May 1781, Hardiman acknowledges sale to Cato West; FHL microfilm 825,510. Loudoun Co., Va., Deed Book N:511, Cato West of Sullivan Co., N.C. to "Brother Charles West," 11 March 1782; FHL microfilm 32,303.

[143] Jefferson County., Miss., Chancery Court, probate packet A-79, W[illiam]. West; FHL microfilm 1,888,885: 23 July 1810, Sarah West, Thomas West, and Zachariah Kirkland administrators; 6 September 1827, William E. Parker admr., "in rite of his wife Sarah Parker (formerly Sarah West)." Receipts in this probate packet show James Raiford West was William's son, not Cato's son as appeared on DAR supplemental application national no. 426446+430. Catahoula Parish, La., Deed Book C:310, no. 558C, heirs of Zachariah Kirkland include William E. Parker in right of wife Sarah Parker, formerly Sarah Kirkland, 18 March 1828; FHL microfilm 871,307.

[144] *Nashville and Louisville Christian Advocate*, 16 March 1854, v.18, no.12, whole no. 905, fourth page of unpaged newspaper; photocopy from Lambuth University Library. An online genealogical site (http://wc.rootsweb. ancestry.com/cgi-bin/igm.cgi?op=REG&db=blackman-farmer&id=I223824) gives a full marriage date of 10 February 1804, but the contributor did not have citation available for the source that gave the full date (email from Franklin Farmer, 8 February 2010).

[145] "Record of Marks and Brands," Jefferson Co., Miss., Deed Book A2:74, 5 August 1803, Wm West, ⊤W (annotated to include Wm. Parker, WP, likely in 1811); marks of the ears: left ear, crop & under bitt; right ear, crop & under bitt; A2:75, 16 August 1803, Cato West, CW, no ear marks; FHL microfilm 892,552.

[146] *FamilySearch* (www.familysearch.org), "Mississippi territorial census: RG 2, series 497, 1801-1816," digital images, Territorial census, Box 17981, Jefferson County, 1805, digital film 4822295, image 100, William West; citing MDAH, Jackson, Mississippi. William West, 1 male over twenty-one, 1 male under twenty-one, 1 female total, 7 slaves.

[147] *FamilySearch* (www.familysearch.org), "Mississippi territorial census: RG 2, series 497, 1801-1816," digital images, Territorial census, Box 17981, Jefferson County, 1808, digital film 4822295, image 116, William West; citing MDAH, Jackson, Mississippi. William West: 2 white males under age twenty-one; 2 white males over twenty-

Cole's Creek originally surveyed for Richard Trevillion in 1788, and sold to West by Manuel Texada in 1798.[148] The William West family composition continued to include two young males in 1810.[149]

William West died intestate sometime before 23 July 1810, when the court recorded his estate's administrators as the widow Sarah (Kirkland) West, Zachariah Kirkland (Sarah's brother), and Thomas West (William's brother); witnessed by Archelaus Kirkland and E(dward). Turner (the decedent's brother-in-law).[150] On 28 August 1810 an inventory of William West's estate recorded his effects, valued at $4,276.56 ¼.[151] The inventory listed five adult slaves, which matched his 1810 territorial census entry, but also listed four additional young slaves.[152]

The following year, the Register of the Orphans Court of Jefferson County issued a marriage license on "28th June 1811" to the widowed Sarah (Kirkland) West and county judge William E. Parker, permitting them to be married "agreeably to a decree lately obtained for that purpose."[153] However, the recorded marriage return states that Thomas Hinds, chief justice of the county court, had married them three days earlier, on the "twenty fifth day of June 1811."[154] William E. Parker was born 7 November 1786, according to his tombstone.[155]

The remarried Sarah (Kirkland) West Parker resided with her second husband in Harrisonburg near Sicily Island in Catahoula Parish, Louisiana, from about 1817 to 1827,[156] during which time William E. Parker served in the Louisiana House of Representatives.[157] In 1826, a Natchez newspaper carried a notice in several issues: "William E. Parker wishing to move to Mississippi

---

one; 0 females under twenty-one; 1 white female over twenty-one; 0 Jefferson County; 5 total whites; 0 free persons of color; 7 slaves; 12 total inhabitants.

[148] Jefferson Co., Miss., Deed Book A2:45, Manuel Garcia de Texada to Cato West, 7 March 1798; Deed Book B1:280 (201 typed), Cato West conveyed, for love and affection to son William West the tract William then lived on, 264 arpents (about 223 acres) on Cole's Creek, 25 July 1808; FHL microfilm 892,552.

[149] *FamilySearch* (www.familysearch.org), "Mississippi territorial census: RG 2, series 497, 1801-1816," digital images, Territorial census, Box 85>Jefferson County, 1810, digital film 4822299, image 13, William West; citing MDAH, Jackson, Mississippi. William West: 1 white male over age twenty-one; 2 white males under twenty-one; 1 white female over twenty-one; 0 white females under twenty-one; 4 total whites, 0 free persons of color; 5 slaves (this county's schedule is missing the final total inhabitants column seen in Baldwin and Claiborne Counties).

[150] Jefferson Co., Miss., Chancery Court, probate packet A-79, W[illiam]. West, administrators' bond, 23 July 1810; FHL microfilm 1,888,885. All original signatures on this bond.

[151] Jefferson Co., Miss., Probate Records, A2, (page number illegible), inventory of William West estate, 28 August 1810, recorded 30 January 1811; FHL microfilm 893,041.

[152] Ibid. Slaves inventoried as of 28 August 1810: Men: Ned and Jack; Women: Sall, Liddy, Lucy; Girls: Mindon(?), Philis; Boys: Peter, Suba(?).

[153] Jefferson Co., Miss., Marriage Licenses and Certificates, vol. A:93, Parker-West; FHL microfilm 893,070.

[154] Ibid.

[155] Lucien L. McNees, transcriber, *Holmes County Cemetery Records* (N.pl.: n.pub., 1955), 120, "Salem Cemetery, Tolarsville."

[156] Catahoula Parish, La., Conveyance Book B:378-381, no.131B, William E. Parker, Sicily Island land purchase; FHL microfilm 871,307; Conveyance Book C:307, no.584C, William E. Parker and wife sold Sicily Island land; FHL microfilm 871,307. 1820 U.S. census, LA, Catahoula Parish, Harrisonburg, p.19; NARA microfilm M33, roll 31.

[157] David R. Poynter Legislative Research Library, Louisiana House of Representatives, "Membership in the Louisiana House of Representatives 1812-2020" (revised 2019), 63: 1822-1826, William E. Parker; pdf image (http://house.louisiana.gov/H_PDFdocs/HouseMembership_History_CURRENT.pdf).

wants to sell 640 acre property on Sicily Island (Catahoula Parish), La."[158] Later in 1826, Sarah's son by first husband William West—James Raiford West—married a Connecticut woman,[159] and signed a receipt for his portion of his late father's estate on 6 September 1827.[160]

Between 1827 and 1840, William E. Parker patented ten public land tracts in the part of Yazoo County, Mississippi, that became Holmes County in 1833, and his wife patented three more tracts after his death, all in Township 14 North, Range 1 East and Range 1 West, Choctaw Meridian.[161] Parker served as Judge of the Yazoo County Probate Court until resigning that position prior to 15 December 1831.[162] Not yet age fifty, Parker drafted his will in 1835:

> I, William E. Parker, of Holmes County and State of Mississippi do make and ordain this my last will and testament in the manner and form following—to wit—First, It is my will and wish that my just debts be paid. Second, All my estate both real and personal and of whatever nature and kind so ever and whether in the state of Mississippi or elsewhere—I give and bequeath to my beloved wife Sarah, to use and dispose of in any way she may think proper during her natural life and at her death to my step-son James R. West to him and his legal heirs or assigns forever. Third, I do hereby nominate, constitute, and appoint my beloved wife Sarah sole executrix of this my last will and testament. In testimony whereof I have hereunto set my hand and affixed my seal, the sixth day of November in the year of our Lord one thousand eight hundred and thirty five (1835).
>
> Wm. E. Parker[163]

William E. Parker died within a month of writing his will in 1835.[164] His remains were interred in the Salem Cemetery where two of his wife's toddler grandchildren—Sarah Elizabeth West and Martha Annie West—had been buried the year before.[165] The cemetery in Section 20, Township 14 North, Range 1 East of the Choctaw Meridian straddles the line separating the tracts patented by Daniel Swayze, one of the witnesses to his will, and by Ann (West) Winn Deloach, his wife's former sister-in-law.

---

[158] "Advertisements," *The Ariel* (Natchez, Miss.), 6 February 1826, v.1, no.29, p.8, col.2.

[159] *Boston Traveler* (Boston, Mass.), 25 August 1826, v.2, no.16, p.3, col.2, "Marriages": "In Wethersfield, James R. West, Esq., of Harrisonburg, Louisiana, to Miss Elizabeth D. Wright."

[160] Jefferson Co., Miss., Chancery Court, probate packet A-79, W[illiam]. West; FHL microfilm 1,888,885. Although the presence of two young boys in their earlier territorial census records suggests that William West and Sarah Kirkland had two sons, only James Raiford West survived to the time that William West's estate was settled.

[161] U.S. Bureau of Land Management, "Patent Search," database, General Land Office Records (http://www.glorecords.blm.gov/PatentSearch), entries for William Parker, Mount Salus Land Office, docs. no. 243, 5856-5859, 17090-17091, 21007; Jackson Land Office, docs. no. 2492, 2493; and for Sarah Parker, Mount Salus Land Office, doc. no. 27442, and Jackson Land Office docs. no. 28034, and 29988. 1830 U.S. census, Yazoo Co., Miss., p.293 written and stamped, Wm. E. Parker; NARA microfilm M19, roll 71. The surnames of individuals enumerated before and after "Wm. E. Parker" match the surnames of Parker's neighboring patentees of land in T14N R1E: Land, Par[r]isot, Tipton, and Harland.

[162] *Journal of the House of Representatives, of the State of Mississippi at their Fourteenth Session, held in the town of Jackson* (Jackson: printed by Peter Isler, 1830), 221.

[163] Holmes County, Miss., Will Book 1:151-152, William E. Parker, 6 November 1835, recorded December Term 1835; Chancery Clerk, Lexington. Witnesses Daniel D. Swayze, John D. Nixon, Parmenus Howard, E. Mirancy.

[164] Ibid.

[165] McNees, *Holmes County Cemetery Records* (1955), 120.

Sarah (Kirkland) West Parker survived her second husband by nearly 20 years. Her obituary furnished much detail on her life, likely provided to its author, Rev. Richard Abbey, by her only known child, Rev. James Raiford West:

> For the Advocate
> Mrs. Sarah Parker, of this vicinity, is no more. She was born in Fairfield, South Carolina, March 12, 1787, and died, at her residence in Holmes county, Miss., Feb. 17, 1854, having almost closed her sixty-seventh year. She was married to Mr. William West in 1803, and became a widow in 1809. In 1811, she was again married to Judge Wm. E. Parker, who died, at their late residence, in 1835, and by the side of whose dust her own remains were deposited two days since.
> Sister Parker was the mother of Rev. James R. West, who was, a considerable time, a member of the Mississippi Conference, now a local elder in our church, and one of our most prominent and substantial citizens.
> She joined the Methodist Episcopal Church in 1830, since which time she has lived a Bible Christian, in the true and full meaning of that term. Scrupulously and conscientiously exact in the discharge of religious duty, she knew no difference between those which are esteemed large, and those which are called small duties. She followed the Saviour fully. One of the most remarkable traits in her character, was mildness, patience, equanimity of temper; and yet she has been heard to say, the only sin she was conscious of, was impatience. Her house was the preacher's home, and she was the preacher's friend. The scope of deep bereavement occasioned by her death is wide; for she was the beloved of many. Truly a mother in Israel is fallen.
> And as she lived, so she died—a Christian. In life she triumphed over sin, and in death she triumphed over death. Sometimes she said, "Don't weep for me; I am happy; I am going right to heaven." A few hours before she died, and when she had been unable to speak for near two days, brother West said to her, "Ma, if all is well, and the way bright before you, press my hand." She opened her eyes of more than life-like brightness, and said, quite audibly, "All is well with me—surely all is well—all is well." She then inquired if they wished anything more. "Give us your blessing," said her son. She then raised her two hands, and prayed audibly for the space of one or two minutes, for him, his wife, and children, and for his son, and his wife and children, as they all gathered around her, and then sunk away to commune no more with earth.
> One of the most affecting funerals scenes I ever witnessed, was as the family and servants crowded the parlor to take a last look at the departed. The blacks were many of them wild and frantic with grief. As they fell to the floor, and cried aloud, their sobs and wailings would have wrung tears from the hardest heart.
> Thus lived and died sister Parker—beloved and mourned—a lady truly—a Christian woman—nothing more—nothing less. R. Abbey. Yazoo City, Feb. 20, 1854. The *Southern Christian Advocate*, and papers at Columbia, South Carolina, are requested to copy.[166]

---

[166] *Nashville and Louisville Christian Advocate*, 16 March 1854, v.18, no.12, whole no. 905, fourth page of unpaginated issue.

The child of William[4] West and Sarah Kirkland:

    i.   JAMES RAIFORD[5] WEST, born 8 January 1805,[167] Jefferson Co., M.T. Married Elizabeth D. Wright, 16 August 1826, Wethersfield, Hartford Co., Conn.[168] Died 21 November 1856, Holmes County, Miss.[169] Children: *(a)* William P., ca.1827-1856[170]; *(b)* Sarah Elizabeth, 24 April 1830-12 August 1834[171]; *(c)* Martha Annie, December 1832-28 June 1834[172]; *(d)* James Raiford Isaac, 22 August 1836-29 April 1843[173]; *(e)* Edwin Wright, January 1838-12 September 1838[174]; *(f)* Frances Sarah, 1839-1907[175]; and *(g)* Lucy R., 1843-1921.[176]

---

[167] McNees, *Holmes County Cemetery Records* (1955), 120. This tombstone is attributed in the published transcription to "Mrs. Raiford D. West" but the dates confirm that it belonged to James R. West.

[168] *Boston Traveler* (Boston, Mass.), 25 August 1826, p.3. Barbour Collection: J. R. West of Harrisonburg, La., married Elizabeth D. Wright of Wethersfield, married 16 August 1826 by Rev. C. J. Terry.

[169] McNees, *Holmes County Cemetery Records* (1955), 120. This death date is incorrectly attributed to his wife, as confirmed in an obituary for Rev. West published on page 2 of *The Weekly American Banner* on 28 November 1856; MDAH microfilm 29697: "Death of a Good Man—It becomes our painful duty to record the death of one of our best citizens and friends. James Raiford West is no more. He died on Friday the 21st inst., at this plantation in Holmes county, the home of his late lamented mother, Mrs. Parker...."

[170] *Weekly American Banner* (Yazoo, Miss.), 11 January 1856, v.1, no.31, p.4, col.5. Details of the attack on William P. West that resulted in his death can be found in *Reports of Cases Argued and Determined by the High Court of Errors and Appeals for the State of Mississippi*, vol. 33 (Philadelphia: T. & J. W. Johnson & Co., 1859), 383-389: Lewis Ogle v. The State of Mississippi.

[171] McNees, *Holmes County Cemetery Records* (1955), 120, "Salem Cemetery, Tolarsville, Miss.": "Sarah Eliz., dau. of J.R. & E.D. West, d. Aug. 12, 1834, age 4 yrs. & 3 mo. & 18 da."

[172] Ibid., "Martha Annie, dau. of J.R. & E.D. West, d. June 28, 1834, age 1 yr. & 6 mo."

[173] *The Yazoo Whig and Political Register* (Yazoo City, Miss.), 13 May 1842, v.6, no.44, p.3, col.1. Birth date calculated from age at death: "aged 6 years, 8 months and 7 days." Obituary confirms burial in the Salem Cemetery.

[174] McNees, *Holmes County Cemetery Records*, 120, "Salem Cemetery, Tolarsville, Miss."

[175] *Find a Grave* (www.findagrave.com), Fanny Christmas, 1844-1907, memorial 24557968 by Ron Manley; photograph (Roseland Cemetery, Amite Co., Miss.). 1850 U.S. census, Yazoo Co., Miss., p.525 stamped, p.90 written, dwelling 856, family 890; F.S. West age ten or eleven, so tombstone birth year of 1844 likely incorrect; NARA microfilm M432, roll 382. "Southern Claims Commission Approved Claims, 1871-1880," Claim 13748, James R. West estate, Holmes County, Mississippi; NARA, Record Group 217; photocopies of original. Fannie's deposition, dated 6 September 1873, appears on pages hand-numbered 6 and 7 of the 80-page file.

[176] 1850 U.S. census, Yazoo Co., Miss., p.525 stamped, p.90 written, dwelling 856, family 890; L. R. West age eight; NARA microfilm M432, roll 382. "Southern Claims Commission Approved Claims, 1871-1880," Claim 13748, James R. West est.; Lucy/Lucie [signed both ways] R. Christmas gave depositions on 3 November 1874 and on 4 March 1878. The file also includes transcriptions of her marriage record. She claimed to be born in Holmes County; claimed her closest Union relatives would be first cousins, her mother's relatives in Connecticut; during war she was 15 and at school; supported Union because her mother was a "Union woman"; one of their old servants told Union forces that had occupied Yazoo City about their Union sympathies ("a company of them procured a sack of coffee and sent it to my Mother"); she married in Holmes County on 29 December 1863, husband Harry/Henry Christmas was an Assistant Surgeon in the hospital at Richmond. In her later deposition she described the heirs of J. R. West besides herself and sister Fanny as "my brother's children; [struck out: "who was killed in 1856"] the oldest named Betty, I do not know her age exactly; J. R. West, Willie West, and Emma West. I do not know their ages. They were children during the war." Her mother died "In May 1867." *Find a Grave* (www.findagrave.com), Lucy R. Christmas, 1843-1921, memorial 14021214 by "NatalieMaynor"; photograph (Odd Fellows Cemetery, Holmes Co., Miss.).

6. MARTHA ELIZABETH[4] WEST (*Cato[3], William[2,1]*), daughter of Cato West and Martha Wills Green,[177] was born in the Natchez District 1782-1784[178] and, thus, age sixteen to eighteen when she married Lt. JOHN ALEXANDER DAVIDSON (son of Brig. Gen. William Lee Davidson and Elizabeth Mary Brevard)[179] in Pickering (later Jefferson) County on 6 May 1800:

> Married - On the 6th inst. at Cole's Creek, Lieut. John A. Davidson of the U.S. Army, to Miss Martha West, daughter of Cato West, Esq.[180]

Cato West conveyed a 350-French-acre tract on Cole's Creek "for love and affection" to this son-in-law "and family" in 1802.[181] Less than a year later, Martha died.[182] No children Martha may have had prior to her death appear to have survived, although there is a second female in John's 1805 Jefferson County household that may be a short-lived daughter;[183] the other female was his second wife, Elizabeth (Green) Hutchins (daughter of Thomas Marston Green and Martha Kirkland[184] and divorced wife of John Hutchins).[185] Their first son,[186] Thomas Green

---

[177] Gloria Lambert Kerns, *Early Newspapers of Natchez, Mississippi, 1800-1828* (Shreveport, La.: J&W Enterprises, 1993), 1, citing *Green's Impartial Observer*, 19 May 1800: "...Miss Martha West, daughter of Cato West, Esq."

[178] [Census of the District of Natchez], 1784; Papeles Procedentes de la isla de Cuba, legajo 116, folio 519, sixteenth entry on page; Clayton Library, Houston. One female added since 1782 census.

[179] Rowan County, North Carolina, Marriage Bonds, vol. D, image 47, Davidson-Brevard, 10 December 1767; FHL microfilm 500,952. Rowan Co., N.C., Will Book B:11-14, William Lee Davidson, 17 December 1780; FHL microfilm 313,801: "wife Mary...sons...John Alexander Davidson, Ephraim Brevard Davidson...." Logan County, Kentucky., Will Book C:44, (remarried widow) Mary Harris, 26 December 1823; FHL microfilm 364,609: "son John A. Davidson...grandchildren... [who are] children of Ephraim B. Davidson, dec'd...."

[180] Kerns, *Early Newspapers of Natchez, Mississippi, 1800-1828* (1993), 1, citing *Green's Impartial Observer*, 19 May 1800. This Pickering County marriage is recorded in Jefferson County, Mississippi, Deed Book A1:30, Davidson-West, 1800; FHL microfilm 892,552.

[181] Jefferson Co., Miss., Deed Book A2:2, Cato West to son-in-law John A. Davidson, 22 June 1802; FHL microfilm 892,552: Cato to son-in-law John A. Davidson and family, for love and affection, 350 French acres granted to Scriber in 1793, sold by Norsworthy Hunter to Cato West on south side of north fork of Cole's Creek.

[182] John A. Davidson remarried on 19 May 1803, to Elizabeth Green; Jefferson Co., Miss., Deeds A2:77, recorded 1 September 1803; FHL microfilm 892,552.

[183] *FamilySearch* (www.familysearch.org), "Mississippi territorial census: RG 2, series 497, 1801-1816," digital images, Territorial census, Box 17981, Jefferson County, 1805, digital film 4822295, image 98, John A. Davidson; citing MDAH, Jackson, Mississippi.

[184] Jefferson Co., Miss., Will Book A:4, Thomas Marston Green, 5 December 1812; FHL microfilm 893,068. Green family Bible transcription in supporting documentation for NSDAR nat. no. 373,979, p.2: "Thomas Marston Green, Jr. married Martha Kirkland, Feb. 15, 1780," their child Elizabeth Green born "18 January 1783"; p.3: "Elizabeth Green married Mr. Hutchins, 2. John Davidson."

[185] *Sargent's Code: a Collection of the Original Laws of the Mississippi Territory enacted 1799-1800 by Governor Winthrop Sargent and the Territorial Judges* (Historical Records Survey, 1939), 126: "a law to divorce Elizabeth Hutchins from John Hutchins, her husband," 3 October 1799. "Hutchins, Elizabeth vs. Hutchins, John," no date, Subject File collection, MDAH; title notes: "In a 1799 divorce case, John Hutchins accused his wife Elizabeth Green Hutchins of adultery and of attempted poisoning." *Ancestry* (https://www.ancestry.com/mediaui-viewer/tree/109397206/person/400073224932/media/2f2f4e0a-0d9d-49ff-bd93-6898fe99a993), images 3-29, user-posted PDF of transcriptions of the correspondence, petition, answer, and witnesses' testimony at the September 1799 divorce trial; source not stated but bears the same "Subject File" stamp used by the MDAH.

[186] Jefferson Co., Miss., Will Book A:4, will of Thomas Marston Green, 5 December 1812; FHL microfilm 893,068. The testator identifies Thomas Green Davidson as the eldest son of his daughter Eliza and her husband John Davidson.

Davidson, later served in the U.S. Congress, and his Congressional biography provides information on this family and gives his full birth date as 3 August 1805.[187]

John A. Davidson's father, William Lee Davidson, died in the American Revolution from a gunshot believed to be fired by a Tory guide named Frederick Hager.[188] An undocumented tradition holds that John Davidson, assisted by his uncle Robert Brevard, eventually tracked Hager to New Madrid, Missouri, and killed him in 1805.[189]

After his U.S. Army service, John A. Davidson apparently ran a tavern or "house of public entertainment" in Greenville, Jefferson County, in 1811.[190] He and his family remained in Jefferson County until his death before 26 May 1823, when administration of his estate began.[191] Those records include John M. Pintard's claim for $25, due for a "1 cherry raized lid coffin" he provided in 1823.[192]

The possible child of Martha[4] West and John A. Davidson:

Perhaps i.   (UNKNOWN FEMALE)[5] WEST, born about 1801-1804; died after 1805.

7. MARY[4] WEST (*Cato[3], William[2,1]*), daughter of Cato West and Martha Wills Green,[193] was born in the Natchez District about 1784-1786 if she were age sixteen to eighteen when she was married to EDWARD TURNER (son of Lewis Ellzey Turner and Theodosia Payne)[194] on

[187] Ibid. *Biographical Directory of the American Congress, 1774 to 1949* (Washington, D.C.: Government Printing Office, 1950), 1058: Thomas Green Davidson born 3 August 1805. Thus, John Davidson is presumed to have married his second wife before December 1804, placing the death of the first Mrs. Davidson at some time prior to that date.
[188] Chalmers Gaston Davidson, *Piedmont Partisan–The Life and Times of Brigadier-General William Lee Davidson* (Davidson, N.C.: Davidson College, 1951), 163.
[189] Davidson, *Piedmont Partisan*, 163. However, Hager's contemporary/officer, Gen. Joseph Graham, asserted that Hager, with other "fugitives from justice…made the first American settlement on the Arkansas River, near Six Post, married and raised a family there, and died in the year 1814"; William Alexander Graham, *General Joseph Graham and his Papers on North Carolina Revolutionary History* (Edwards & Broughton, 1904), 294.
[190] "Old Tavern Licenses of Jefferson County, Mississippi," *U.S.GenWeb* (http://jeffersoncountyms.org /taverns.htm); Tavern License Bond, $300, 26 March 1811, Thomas Harding and John A. Davidson "to keep house of public entertainment on the main road"; abstracted by Al Whitehead. The source citation for these licenses is not described. Davidson also signed bond with tavern license applicant Jane Green on 23 March 1812.
[191] *FamilySearch* (www.familysearch.org), "Mississippi territorial census: RG 2, series 497, 1801-1816," digital images, Territorial census, Box 17981, Jefferson County, 1816, digital film 4822295, image 125, John A. Davidson; citing MDAH, Jackson, Mississippi. 1820 U.S. census, Jefferson County, Miss., p.53A written, line 15, John A. Davidson; NARA microfilm M33, roll 58. Jefferson Co., Miss., Chancery Court, probate packet B-182, John A. Davidson; administrators Elizabeth Davidson and Filmer W. Green; FHL microfilm 1,901,538.
[192] Jefferson Co., Miss., Chancery Court, probate packet B-182, John A. Davidson; Pintard claim; FHL microfilm 1,901,538.
[193] *New York Gazette and General Advertiser* (New York, N.Y.), 4 November 1802, v.15, no.5268, p.2, col.3: "…Miss Mary West, daughter of the Hon. Cato West."
[194] Fayette Co., Kentucky, Mixed (Probate) Records, Book B:211, distribution from Edward Payne estate to Mr. Lewis E. Turner and wife, 8 April 1811; FHL microfilm 2,111,465, and Book G:1-6, distribution of Lewis E. Turner estate to Edward Turner, October Court 1824; FHL microfilm 2,111,468. Bible belonging to Mrs. L. P. Conner, Natchez, Miss., Mississippi DAR Genealogical Records Committee, 1934-1936, Series 1, Volume 14:134-136, Theodosia Payne, born 22 January 1751; NSDAR, Seimes Technology Center, Washington, D.C.; hereinafter "Turner family Bible."

5 September 1802 by David Cooper "in pursuance of a license from the Governor of the Territory."[195] A New York newspaper published a notice of the event:

> Marriages, at Natches [*sic*], Edward Turner, Esq., to Miss Mary West, daughter of the Hon. Cato West.[196]

Mary's father Cato West did not convey property to Edward Turner—as he had done for his Davidson son-in-law earlier that year—nor was Edward Turner located in the 1805 territorial census. The 1808 and 1810 territorial censuses of Jefferson County included Edward Turner's household, which included two females under twenty-one years old in both years.[197] In February 1811, Mary (West) Turner died in Palmyra, then Claiborne County, Miss.[198]

Edward Turner married a second time, on 27 December 1812 in Adams County, Miss., to Elizabeth Baker.[199] However, Turner's involvement with the West family continued, in his capacity as a lawyer. Cato West's estate records show that Edward Turner was paid for representing the family in "U.S. v. Cato West's Administrators."[200]

Edward and Mary (West) Turner's only child known to survive to adulthood was Theodosia Lavinia Turner, who married and had two children.[201] A portrait survives of Theodosia and her older child Mary West Griffith, painted by Matthew H. Jouett.[202] However, both of Theodosia's children died before their grandfather Edward Turner wrote his will in 1859. As his will does not provide for or mention either of Theodosia's children or their heirs, it appears that none of Mary (West) Turner's descendants outlived her husband Edward Turner.

> In the Name of God Amen I Edward Turner of the County of Adams and State of Mississippi do make this my last will and testament, revoking all others. Having made such provision for my daughters Mary Louisa & Fanny Elizabeth as my circumstances

---

[195] Jefferson County, Miss., Deed Book A2 (1802-1804):77, Turner-West marriage, recorded 1 September 1803 but solemnized on 5 September 1802; FHL microfilm 892,552. The Turner family Bible transcription listed the date of Edward Turner's marriage to Mary West incorrectly as 5 September *1803*.

[196] *New York Gazette and General Advertiser,* 4 November 1802, v.15, no.5268, p.2, col.3.

[197] *FamilySearch* (www.familysearch.org), "Mississippi territorial census : RG 2, series 497, 1801-1816," digital images, Territorial census, Box 17981, Jefferson County, 1808, digital film 4822295, p.4, image 111, Edward Turner; 1810, digital film 4822299, p.4, image 11, Edward Turner; citing MDAH, Jackson, Mississippi. An Edward Turner entry also appears in the 1810 territorial census of Claiborne County (2 males over twenty-one) which does not appear to pertain to this man although Mary (West) Turner died in 1811 in Palmyra, then considered Claiborne County; Claiborne and Warren Counties, 1810, digital film 4822295, p.3, image 45, Edward Turner; citing MDAH, Jackson, Mississippi.

[198] W. C. Smedes and T. A. Marshall, Reporters, "Sketch of the Life of the Hon. Edward Turner," *Reports of Cases Argued and Determined in the High Court of Errors and Appeals for the State of Mississippi* (Boston: Charles C. Little & James Brown, 1844), 10-11. The Turner family Bible gives a full death date of 18 February 1811.

[199] Adams Co., Miss., Marriage Record No. 1, 1802-1819, p. 240, Turner-Baker license, 26 December 1812; FHL microfilm 893,521. Turner family Bible gives marriage date as 27 December 1812.

[200] Jefferson Co., Miss., Chancery Court, probate packet B-98, Cato West Jr. [*sic*]; FHL microfilm 1,889,020. "U.S. District Court, Natchez, Miss., Record Book, 1819-1824," 397-399, 1 January 1822, Records of the District Courts of the United States (RG 21), NA-Atlanta.

[201] However, the Turner family Bible lists a Nathaniel Lewis Turner, born 14 November 1807, next to the entry for Theodosia "Ann" Turner, born 3 June 1810, suggesting there may have been an earlier son who died as an infant. The 1808 territorial census for Edward Turner in Jefferson County did not include any male under age twenty-one.

[202] Patti Carr Black, *Art in Mississippi, 1720-1980* (Jackson, Miss.: University Press of Miss., 1998), 46-47.

from time enabled me to make as will appear from accounts in my Ledger, in my own hand writing, I hereby devise and bequeath to my beloved wife Eliza all the rest & residue of my Estate, real & personal, to have and to hold during her natural life, that is to say, I give to her my personal estate, except the slaves, in fee simple, and the land and slaves, I give to her during her natural life, it being my intention to give to my wife the use of my land and slaves during her life, remainder to my heirs at Law. Provided, that my executors (my wife included) may, at any time, three or a majority of them, my wife being one, may, at any time they may deem proper, sell & convey, all, or any part of my estate, for the payment of my debts, and the better & more convenient support of my wife, and & they are hereby constituted Trustees for that purpose. The proceeds of sale, to be invested in such manner as to [neave?] to my wife the sum of from three to five thousand dollars per annum for her support & maintenance. And I do hereby constitute and appoint my beloved wife, & my friends John T. McMurran, Lemuel [J.?] Conner, & Henry Turner (my nephew) of Palmyra, Mississippi) Executors & Trustees of this my last will & testament. And it is further my will, that my said Executors, shall not be required to give security, for the administration of my Estate.

Given under my hand & seal this fifth day of November, A.D. 1859.

E. Turner [signature] {seal}

[no witnesses]

State of Mississippi	In the Probate Court of said county
Adams County	At the May Term A.D. 1860 thereof

In the matter of a certain instrument of writing purporting to be the last will and testament of Edward Turner, deceased:

Personally appeared in open Court, at the above stated term, William T. Martin and Ralph North, having first been duly sworn, severally deposed and said, that they were well acquainted with the handwriting of Edward Turner, having often seen him write and sign his name, and that the whole of the foregoing instrument of writing, dated the fifth day of November A.D. 1859, as well as the signature thereto, is in the proper handwriting of the said Edward Turner, now deceased, and purporting to be his last will and testament.

Sworn to and subscribed in open Court the 31st day of May A.D. 1860.

Will T. Martin [signature]

Rich'd. A. Inge, Clerk   Ralph North [signature]

Filed May 31, 1860 for probate
Rich'd. A. Inge Clerk
Proved by the testimony of William T. Martin and Ralph North to be wholly in the handwriting of Edward Turner admitted to probate and ordered to be recorded as the last will and testament of said Edward Turner, now deceased.

May Term 1860.   R. Bullock [Jurat?][203]

No tombstone for Mary (West) Turner has been located.

The children of Mary[4] West and Edward Turner:

---

[203] Adams County, Miss., Will Book 3:146, will of Edward Turner, 5 November 1859, proved and recorded 31 May 1860; FHL microfilm 886,245.

i. MARTHA ANN[5] TURNER, b.ca.1803; d.15 June 1809; "Departed this life on Thursday evening the 15th inst., Martha Anne Turner, infant daughter of Edward Turner, Esq., of Greenville, Jefferson County."[204]

ii. THEODOSIA LAVINIA TURNER, b.ca.1805; married William B. Griffith on 12 May 1823;[205] died 9 February 1829; "Died…on the 9th inst., after a short illness, Mrs. Theodosia L. Griffith, widow of the late Wm. B. Griffith, and daughter of the Hon. Edward Turner."[206] Neither of her two children left descendants: *(a)* Martha West: "Died, On the 28th ult. at the residence of L. Baker, Esq. in the city of New York, after a short and severe illness, in the 14th year of her age, Mary West Griffith, daughter of the late Wm. Griffith, of Natchez, and granddaughter of the Hon. Edward Turner, of this county"[207]; *(b)* William Edward Turner: "On the afternoon of the 3rd instant, at the residence of his grandfather, the Hon. Edward Turner in Franklin county, Miss., William E. T. Griffith, late a member of the Bar of this city, aged 24 years. Although but a short time engaged in the active business of his profession, his intelligence and gentlemanly bearing had won the high esteem of his brother practitioners, and endeared him to a large circle of personal friends. The members of the Bar are respectfully desired to meet at the room of the Supreme Court This Morning at 11 o'clock to express the respect in which he was held by them, and their sympathy with the affliction of his family at his untimely loss."[208]

8. THOMAS[4] WEST (*Cato[3], William[2,1]*), son of Cato West and Martha Wills Green,[209] was born before 1787 in the Natchez District.[210] In 1808, Thomas recorded his cattle brand,[211] and in 1815, his father Cato West conveyed to him for love and affection 427 acres on both sides of Cole's Creek that Thomas then occupied and planted, adjoining the tracts of Thomas Calvit, the late Thomas M. Green, and John Vandevall.[212] This constituted part of a 1,238 37/100-acre tract granted to Cato West in 1789,[213] and later designated by the U.S. General Land Office as part of

---

[204] *The Natchez Weekly Democrat* (Natchez, Miss.), 24 June 1809, v.1, no.51, p.3, col.1.

[205] Turner family Bible.

[206] *Southern Galaxy* (Natchez, Miss.), 12 February 1829, v.1, no.38, p.3, col.2.

[207] *The Mississippi Daily Free Trader and Natchez Daily Gazette* (Natchez, Miss.), 11 June 1838, v.1, no.139, p.2, col.5.

[208] *The Daily Picayune* (New Orleans, Louisiana), 6 June 1851, v.15, no.114, p.2, col.5.

[209] Jefferson Co., Miss., Deed Book C1:168, Cato West to "his son, Thomas West," 28 August 1815.

[210] The 1787 Natchez census recorded just one non-adult male in Cato West's household, presumed to be son William, so Thomas likely born just after this time. Thomas would be one of the three boys enumerated, along with three girls, in Cato West's household in the 1792 territorial census of Villa Gayoso (later Jefferson County). See also 1808 and 1810 territorial census entries: *FamilySearch* (www.familysearch.org), "Mississippi territorial census: RG 2, series 497, 1801-1816," digital images, Territorial census, Box 17981, Jefferson County, 1808, digital film 4822295, p.3, image 110, Thomas West; 1810, digital film 4822299, ninth page, image 16, Thomas West; citing MDAH, Jackson, Mississippi.

[211] "Record of Marks and Brands," Jefferson County, Mississippi, Deeds A2:131, 22 September 1808, Thomas West, TW, "Marks of the Ear," left ear: smooth crop & under bit; right ear: overbit & a smo[o]th crop.

[212] Jefferson Co., Miss., Deed Book C1:168; Cato West to son Thomas West, 1 July 1815, recorded 28 August 1815 (includes plat); FHL microfilm 892,553.

[213] U.S. Congress, *American State Papers: Documents, Legislative and Executive of the Congress of the United States in Relation to the Public Lands*, 5 vols. Walter Lowrie, ed. (Washington, D.C.: Duff Green, 1834), 1:776, certificate A27 issued 19 April 1805.

Section 11 of Township 9 North, Range 1 West of the Washington Meridian.[214] On 18 March 1816, Thomas sold 100 acres "bounded on west by brother Charles, on south by Cole's Creek, and all other sides vacant," to his father for $1,500.[215]

Apparently still in his late twenties, Thomas West had sought medical treatment four times in the month preceding the writing of his last will and testament on 18 August 1818:[216]

> I, Thomas West, of Jefferson
> County in the State of Mississippi, do make and declare the following
> my last Will and Testament, I give and to [sic] my Brother Benjamin
> Franklin West my whole estate, both real and personal, to him
> and his heirs forever—reserving however the payment of my
> Just debts—and e[x]cept so much as may be sufficient for the
> expense for the support and schooling of the orphan boy John
> Ewing for the Term of one year—he now living with me—and
> a horse Bridle and Saddle, worth one hundred and fifty, also a
> becoming suit of cloth[e]s, when he shall arrive at the age of eighteen
> years—for the due execution of this my last Will and Testament
> I do hereby nominate and appoint my brother Charles West and
> my worthy friend William Folkes Executors in confidence that
> they will do all things proper for a due Execution thereof—In
> witness whereof I have hereunto signed my name and caused my
> seal to be placed the 18th day of August in the year of our Lord
> 1818.
>   Thomas West {seal}
> Witnesses John Vandevall, Walter Mackey & Israel Coleman.[217]

Thomas died between 9 October 1818, when Dr. Benjamin Bullen last made a house call,[218] and 12 October 1818, when Henry Siebe accepted payment of $35 for the walnut coffin he made.[219] The court bonded Thomas's brother Charles West as sole executor on 26 October 1818.[220] The inventory showed that Thomas West held three slaves at his death: Colbert age forty-five, Tom age eighteen, and Peter age nine.[221] In the sale account of the estate, executor Charles West noted that he had purchased Colbert and that Robert Cocks had purchased Tom.[222] Peter possibly passed into Benjamin F. West's hands, where Thomas directed the remainder of his

---

[214] Cato West claim, Mississippi, serial no. 013090, Serial Patent Files 1908-1951, Records of the Bureau of Land Management, Record Group 49; National Archives, Washington, D.C. [patent no. 1123194, 8 February 1948, Section 11, T9N, R1W and Section 45, T10N, R1W, Washington Meridian]. The land Cato conveyed to son Thomas in 1815 all fell within Section 11, T9N, R1W.

[215] Jefferson Co., Miss., Deed Book C1:197; Thomas West to Cato West, written and recorded 18 March 1816; FHL microfilm 892,553. Thomas W. West, the grantor's first cousin, signed as one of the three witnesses.

[216] Jefferson Co., Miss., Chancery Court, probate packet B-40, estate of Thomas West; FHL microfilm 1,889,019. Dr. Benjamin Bullen's claim against the estate of Thomas West.

[217] Jefferson Co., Miss., Will Book A:24, will of Thomas West, 18 August 1818, proved date not recorded in the will book; FHL microfilm 893,068. Original will image, FHL microfilm 1,907,066, item 2.

[218] Jefferson Co., Miss., Chancery Court, probate packet B-40, estate of Thomas West, Bullen account; FHL microfilm 1,889,019.

[219] Ibid., Siebe account.

[220] Ibid., executor bonded.

[221] Ibid., slave inventory.

[222] Ibid., slave purchases.

estate not specifically bequeathed to others. John Ewing obtained his "legacy" on 9 August 1826,[223] to which the will entitled him at age eighteen, and Charles West filed the estate's final account on 28 August 1826.[224]

Thomas' burial location has not been documented. However, it may be the two acres on Cole's Creek that his father Cato West reserved, in his will, "as a burying place in common for my family and others forever."[225]

9. ELIZABETH "BETSY"[4] WEST (*Cato³, William²·¹*), daughter of Cato West and Martha Wills Green,[226] was born in the Natchez District 1788-1790[227] and, thus, was about age sixteen to eighteen when she married DR. HEZEKIAH J. BALCH in Jefferson County, M.T., on or after 5 January 1806.[228] The previous year, the household of Dr. Balch (son of Hezekiah James Balch and Martha McCandless)[229] contained two white males over age twenty-one and six slaves.[230]

Just one year into her marriage, Elizabeth died in Greenville, Jefferson Co., M.T., on 25 January 1807:

> Died on Sunday, Mrs. Elizabeth Balch, consort of Dr. H. J. Balch of Greenville.[231]

---

[223] Ibid., Ewing's account, valued at $390.60.

[224] Ibid., final account.

[225] Jefferson Co., Miss., Will Book A:24-25, will of Cato West, 30 July 1818.

[226] Green family Bible transcription in supporting documentation for NSDAR nat. no. 373,979.

[227] The 1787 Natchez census recorded just one non-adult female in Cato West's household, presumed to be daughter Martha, so Elizabeth likely born shortly after this time. Elizabeth would be one of the three girls enumerated, along with three boys, in Cato West's household in the 1792 territorial census of Villa Gayoso (later Jefferson County). Elizabeth would also be one of the six females under twenty-one recorded in the 1805 territorial census of Jefferson County (*FamilySearch* (www.familysearch.org), "Mississippi territorial census : RG 2, series 497, 1801-1816," digital images, Territorial census, Box 17981, Jefferson County, 1805, digital film 4822295, image 100, Cato West; citing MDAH, Jackson, Mississippi). This birth estimate makes Elizabeth about age seventeen when she married.

[228] Jefferson Co., Miss., Marriage Licenses and Certificates, vol. A:17, Hezekiah J. Balch and Betsy West (license only), 5 January 1806; FHL microfilm 893,070. Green family Bible transcription in NSDAR nat. no. 373,979: "Elizabeth married Dr. Baugh [*sic*]."

[229] Only indirect evidence supports this parentage. In his 1816 will, Hezekiah J. Balch devised a slave, "Fann," to his unnamed mother (Jefferson Co., Miss., Will Book A:61-62, Hezekiah J. Balch, 16 July 1816 (probate date not recorded); FHL microfilm 893,068). Receipt of "Fanny" was acknowledged by Samuel C. McWhirter (Jefferson Co., Miss., Chancery Court, probate packet B-17, H. S.[*sic*] Balch; FHL microfilm 1,889,018). Samuel was the son of George McWhirter (Wilson Co., Tennessee, Wills and Inventories 1832-1839, "1837-1839," 33-34; FHL microfilm 430,843). Compiled information (https://wc.rootsweb.com/cgi-bin/igm.cgi?op=GET&db=judyk&id=14681) claims McWhirter attended college with Hezekiah Balch Sr., who died in 1776 in Mecklenburg County, North Carolina (Mecklenburg Co., N.C., Court Minutes 1774-1785:81, Martha Balch, administratrix, third Tuesday in January 1777; FHL microfilm 19,310), and married Balch's widow there on 29 September 1782 (http://lady3248.tripod.com/mcwhortergenealogy.htm). George "McWhorter's" Revolutionary War pension application states that his family Bible proves his age, and this may be the source for full dates and places appearing in otherwise undocumented Balch genealogies: *Fold3* (https://www.fold3.com/image/ 24231503), interrogatories of claimant George McWhorter, 25 May 1833, North and South Carolina service, pension application no. S9011, Revolutionary War Pension and Bounty-Land-Warrant Application Files; NARA microfilm M804, roll 1701.

[230] *FamilySearch* (www.familysearch.org), "Mississippi territorial census: RG 2, series 497, 1801-1816," digital images, Territorial census, Box 17981, Jefferson County, 1805, digital film 4822295, image 99, p.4, Hezekiah J. Balch; citing MDAH, Jackson, Mississippi.

[231] *Mississippi Messenger* (Natchez, Miss.), Tuesday, 27 January 1807, v.3, no.126, p.2, col.4.

Elizabeth may have given birth to a son, as Hezekiah's entry in the 1808 territorial census of Jefferson County included one white male under age twenty-one.[232] Earlier that year, Hezekiah had remarried, to his late wife's first cousin MARY WEST (daughter of Charles West and Sarah Withers),[233] on 10 January 1808 in Adams Co., M.T., so the young male is not likely to be a child of the second marriage.[234] A young white male continued to be enumerated in Hezekiah's Jefferson County household in 1810.[235] The young male does not appear in Hezekiah's household in 1816,[236] in which year Hezekiah lost his second wife on 7 May:

> Died, in the neighborhood of Greenville, Jefferson county, on Tuesday evening the 7th instant, after a long and painful illness, which she sustained with [C]hristian fortitude, Mrs. MARY BALCH, in the 24th year of her age.[237]

Two months later, Hezekiah wrote his last will and testament.[238] His will does not mention any surviving children:

> I, Hezekiah J. Balch of the county of Jefferson and Mississippi Territory do make this my last will and testament in manner and form following to wit, First it is my will that my property be kept together for two or more years at the discretion of my executors hereafter to be named, and conducted and managed by him so as to be improved for the benefit of my heirs and out of the proceeds thereof to pay all my just debts.

> Secondly, I give to my beloved mother my negro woman Fan during her natural life and at her death to revert to my legal heirs. Thirdly, I give to my friend Sarah Parker a feather bed marked Mariah W. West.

> Fourthly, I give to my friend William E. Parker five hundred dollars in cash to be made out of the proceeds of my property as first above mentioned.

---

[232] *FamilySearch* (www.familysearch.org), "Mississippi territorial census: RG 2, series 497, 1801-1816," digital images, Territorial census, Box 17981, Jefferson County, 1808, digital film 4822295, image 108, p.1, Hezekiah J. Balch; citing MDAH, Jackson, Mississippi: 1 male over age 21, 1 male under age 21; 1 female under age 21, 2 slaves, 5 total.

[233] *FamilySearch* (www.familysearch.org), "Original Spanish Record, 1781-1796," Spanish records, vol. 31-32 1795, vol. 32:322-325, original "testimento de Dr. Carlos West," 1 September 1795, 17 September 1795; FHL microfilm 893,509. Fauquier Co., Va., Marriage Bonds and Returns, Vol 1:143, West-Withers, 10 June 1785; FHL microfilm 31,633.

[234] Adams Co., Miss., Marriage Book 1:51-52, Hezekiah J. Balch and "Maria" West, license issued 4 January 1808 (with consent from Maria West's guardian (and stepfather) William Lemon); FHL microfilm 893,521.

[235] *FamilySearch* (www.familysearch.org), "Mississippi territorial census: RG 2, series 497, 1801-1816," digital images, Territorial census, Box 85, Jefferson County, 1810, digital film 4822299, image 18, p.11, Hezekiah Balch; citing MDAH, Jackson, Mississippi: 1 male over age 21, 1 male under age 21; 1 female under twenty-one, 3 slaves, 7 total.

[236] *FamilySearch* (www.familysearch.org), "Mississippi territorial census: RG 2, series 497, 1801-1816," digital images, Territorial census, Box 17981, Jefferson County, 1816, digital film 4822295, image 122, p.1, H. J. Balch; citing MDAH, Jackson, Mississippi: 2 males over twenty-one, 1 female over twenty-one, 3 slaves, 7 total [incorrect total].

[237] *Washington Republican and Natchez Intelligencer* (Natchez, Miss.), Wednesday, 15 May 1816, v.4, no.4, p.3, col. 3.

[238] Jefferson Co., Miss., Will Book A:61-62, Hezekiah J. Balch, 16 July 1816 (probate date not recorded); FHL microfilm 893,068.

Fifthly, all the balance of my estate both real and personal I give and bequeath unto my beloved sister Ann Caldwell during her natural life and at her death to descend to her children to be equally divided amongst them share and share alike to them and their heirs legally begotten forever.

Sixthly, I do hereby nominate, constitute and appoint William E. Parker the sole executor of this my last will and testament in testimony whereof I have hereunto set my hand and affixed my seal this sixteenth day of July 1816.

Hezekiah J. Balch {seal}[239]

The probate file for Dr. Balch's estate includes receipts that help estimate when he died, especially Henry Siebe's bill, for making a "raised lid cherry casket," dated 8 April 1818.[240] The receipts also document the distribution of his estate, including his bequests to his mother and sister. The bulk of Dr. Balch's estate, exceeding $5,000, went to his sister Ann (Balch) Caldwell via her husband Samuel S. Caldwell, who signed a receipt as the agent for H. J. Balch's heirs on 24 February 1819.[241]

The distribution to Ann Caldwell included adult slaves Anthony, Kitty, and Ben, as well as two boys Louis and Charles.[242] The distribution of the enslaved Fanny[243]—and the six-month-old daughter Caroline who had been born to Fanny since Dr. Balch wrote his will—went to Hezekiah's mother, Martha (McCandless) Balch McWhirter, by way of her stepson Samuel C. McWhirter, who signed a receipt therefor on 14 November 1819.[244]

The possible child of Elizabeth[4] West and Dr. Hezekiah L. J. Balch:

Perhaps i.   (MALE)[5] BALCH, b.ca.1807; died before 16 July 1816.[245]

10. CHARLES[4] WEST (*Cato[3], William[2,1]*), son of Cato West and Martha Wills Green,[246] was born about 1791-1793 in the Natchez District.[247] On 22 September 1808, Charles recorded his cattle

---

[239] Ibid.

[240] Jefferson Co., Miss., Chancery Court, probate packet B-17, Hezekiah J. Balch; FHL microfilm 1,889,018.

[241] Ibid.

[242] Ibid. The two slaves named on Balch's inventory not included here are Jack and Fanny.

[243] This may be the Fanny (born about July 1803) that Cato West purchased on 28 April 1804 from Robert Boyce of Kentucky. If so, Fanny was about two months shy of 16 when her daughter Caroline was born about May 1819. Fanny's advanced pregnancy may be the reason she did not go with Mr. Caldwell in February 1819 but rather in November 1819. A recorded conveyance of Fanny from Cato West to daughter Elizabeth "Betsy" West (perhaps upon her marriage to Dr. Balch) has not been located. The fate of Hezekiah's other slave Jack is not known.

[244] Wilson County, Tennessee, Wills and Inventories 1832-1839, "1837-1839," 33-34, will of George McWhirter (identifies his son as Samuel C. McWhirter); FHL microfilm 430,843. Jefferson Co., Miss., Will Book A:61-62, Hezekiah J. Balch, 16 July 1816 (probate date not recorded); FHL microfilm 893,068.

[245] Jefferson Co., Miss. Will Book A:61-62, Hezekiah J. Balch, 1816; the testator did not mention any surviving children.

[246] Jefferson Co., Miss., Will Book A:25, will of Cato West, names "son Charles West" as one of his executors.

[247] 1850 U.S. census, Jefferson Co., Miss., Fayette, p.100 stamped, 199 written, dwelling and family 276, Charles West, age fifty-seven; NARA microfilm M432, roll 374. 1860 U.S. census, Jefferson Co., Miss., Police Dist. 3, p.36 written, dwelling 283, family 294, Charles West, age sixty-nine; NARA microfilm M653, roll 584.

mark.[248] On 28 August 1815, his father Cato conveyed to him, for love and affection, 753 acres on Cole's Creek near the residence of William Fairbanks and adjoining those lands claimed by Thomas Calvit.[249] This conveyance was part of a 1,238 37/100-acre tract granted to Cato West in 1789.[250]

The third-born male, Charles West was about to become the eldest surviving son of Cato West in 1818, when both his father Cato and brother Thomas drafted their wills. Both testators appointed Charles West as one of their executors, an honor that would complicate Charles's life for the foreseeable future and involve him in a federal case.[251] Charles, his stepmother Martha (Harper) West, and Cowles Mead, Esq., served as Cato West's executors.[252] A few items in Cato West's probate file indicate that the widow and stepson were not of one mind on some issues:

> [undated]
> Mr. Cowden,
> D. Sr., I have transcribed the acct against minors as you wished, and have annexed the charges for Board &c & have made an account against the Estate for Board of overseers in 1819 & 20 and Board for Mr. Charles West whilst he was there, and an amount pd him in cash which I have no Doubt he will charge to the Estate. At any rate it is due me either from him or the Estate…
> > William L. Davis[253] [Martha (Harper) West's second husband]

> To Mr. Charles West
> The Pines, Mar. 17, 1824
> Dear Sir:
> I do well recollect that Mrs. Davis, formerly Mrs. West, informed me that it was her wish that you should live with her the first year of her widowhood, for the benefit of your society, and on her account I spoke to you on the subject, stating her wish, and united mine in the opinion that you ought to remain with her.
> > Very respectfully,
> > your Obt. Servt.
> > Cowles Mead[254]

---

[248] "Record of Marks and Brands," Jefferson Co., Miss., Deeds A2:132, 18 June 1812, Charles West (four symbols in brand), marks of the ears: left ear, crop & upper bit; right ear, crop up[p]er bit & slit; FHL microfilm 892,552.

[249] Jefferson Co., Miss., Deed Book C1:169, Cato West to son Charles West, 1 July 1815 (recorded 28 August 1815), includes plat; FHL microfilm 892,553.

[250] U.S. Congress, *American State Papers: Documents, Legislative and Executive of the Congress of the United States*, 5 vols. Walter Lowrie, ed. (Washington, D.C.: Duff Green, 1834), 1:776. Cato West claim, Mississippi, serial no. 013090, Serial Patent Files 1908-1951, RG 49; NA-Washington [patent no. 1123194, 8 February 1948, Section 11, T9N, R1W and Section 45, T10N, R1W, Washington Meridian]. The land Cato conveyed to son Charles in 1815 comprised all of Section 45, T10N, R1W, and part of Section 11, T9N, R1W.

[251] U.S. vs. Cato West's executors, "U.S. District Court, Natchez, Miss., Record Book, 1819-1824," 397-399, Records of the District Courts of the United States (RG 21), NA-Atlanta (referenced in Jefferson Co., Miss., Chancery Court, probate packet no. B-98, Cato West Jr. [*sic*]).

[252] Jefferson Co., Miss., Will Book A:24-25, wills of Thomas West and Cato West; FHL microfilm 893,068.

[253] Jefferson Co., Miss., Chancery Court, probate packet B-98, Cato West Jr. [*sic*]; FHL microfilm 1,889,020. Davis letter.

[254] Ibid., Mead letter.

Charles West married CHARLOTTE E. NEELY (parentage as yet undocumented) on 6 June 1820 in Jefferson Co., Miss.[255] Either the author or transcriber of the Green family Bible's listing of the children of Cato West and Martha Wills Green apparently combined two children into one, listing "Claborne" West, rather than Charles West, as the son who married Charlotte "Neilley."[256]

The 1820 federal census of Jefferson County, taken as of the first Monday in August, lists a Charles West household with a male age ten to sixteen, a male twenty-six to forty-five, and a female sixteen to twenty-six.[257] The composition of the household suggests the possibility that the young male was either of his younger brothers Richard or Benjamin, for whom he was guardian. The 1830 and 1840 households enumerated for Charles West continue to include a male born about 1800-1810, but also a female significantly older than Charles.[258]

Charles's wife died on 31 August 1838 and was buried in the Fayette Cemetery.[259]

> DIED—On the evening of the 31st Aug., at her late residence, near Fayette, Jefferson county, Mrs. CHARLOTTE WEST, consort of Mr. Charles West—leaving an afflicted husband, five affectionate children and an extensive circle of friends to mourn their irreparable loss. In life she was an affectionate wife, kind and tender mother, a benevolent and accommodating neighbor, and was beloved and highly esteemed by a large circle of friends and acquaintance[s]. Her death will also be felt and greatly lamented by the Church of Christ, of which she had been an exemplary member for several years.
> It is not the lot of every [C]hristian to enjoy the sweet peace of mind and calm composure which characterized the protracted illness of Mrs. West. She was a most patient sufferer, and seemed desirous to live for her family and friends only, and shewed no dread of death, nor feared the judgment bar; so far from it, a few evenings before her dissolution in conversing and meditating on the goodness of God, she was constrained to praise [H]im, and though scare able to speak, attempted to join in a song of praise to that God in whom she had so long trusted. She has, no doubt, joined her first and last born, two lovely babes, that had gone before her. If the mere anticipation of Heaven produces in the dying Christian an anxiety to meet the Lord, while on the bed of affliction, what must the possession of all that is meant my Heaven be—to walk in the golden streets—gaze on

---

[255] Jefferson Co., Miss., Marriage Licenses and Certificates, vol. A:154, West-Neely, 6 June 1820; FHL microfilm 893,070. Same page, and dated one week earlier, Martha West and William L. Davis marriage. Although Charlotte Neely's parentage has not been documented, her sisters are documented as Catherine (Neely) Elam Gibson (Marriages vol. B:44 and B:257) and Caroline (Neely) McCollum (Marriages B:93, FHL microfilm 893,070) per Catherine Gibson's 1885 will, identifying a daughter of Charlotte and a daughter of Caroline as her nieces (Wills B:169, FHL microfilm 893,068).

[256] Green family Bible transcription in supporting documentation for NSDAR nat. no. 373,979, 13. Contemporary documentation shows *Charles* West married Charlotte *Neely*, and Richard *Claborne* West married *Amelia Trahern*.

[257] 1820 U.S. census, Jefferson Co., Miss., p.59; NARA microfilm M33, roll 58.

[258] 1830 U.S. census, Jefferson Co., Miss., p.35; NARA microfilm M19, roll 71. Oldest female age sixty to seventy (born 1760-1770); 1840 U.S. census, Jefferson Co., Miss., p.288; NARA microfilm M704, roll 214. Oldest female age fifty to sixty (born 1780-1790). If the age ranges are slightly off, this female could be Charles's mother-in-law, as a tombstone for a Nelly Neely, interred in Fayette Cemetery next to the Wests, shows died on 16 January 1844 at age 68 (thus born circa 1775); Brown, *Jefferson Co., Miss., Cemeteries, Etc.*, 2:98.

[259] *Find a Grave* (www.findagrave.com), Charlotte E. West, 31 August 1838, memorial 23788122, by "NatalieMaynor"; photograph (Fayette Cemetery, Jefferson Co., Miss.). "Aged 33 years." Brown, *Jefferson Co., Miss., Cemeteries, Etc.*, 2:99.

the uncreated glories of God, bask in the sunshine of his love and live for ever clear of pain or dread of disappointment?

May this dispensation of Providence be blessed abundantly to her kind and sympathetic husband for whom she manifested so much anxiety. May it be regarded by all her surviving friends as a loud and solemn reiteration of the Saviour's voice. *"Be ye also ready."* E.[260]

Marriage and tombstone records help explain the relationships of the individuals in Charles West's 1850 and 1860 households in Fayette, Jefferson Co., Miss.[261] Daughter Frances Jane West had married Dr. John H. Dorsey on 11 April 1850 in Jefferson County,[262] and the newlyweds resided in Charles's household in 1850. In the next ten years, three of Charles's five known children died,[263] and his 1860 household included a widowed daughter-in-law, and grandsons through two different children.[264]

Charles West drafted his will in the spring of 1859, adding a codicil by the end of that summer:

> Exhibit A
> I, Charles West of Jefferson County, and state of Mississippi,
> do make this my last will and testament, revoking hereby all other
> wills by me heretofore made.
> I give to my son Thomas Cato & Martha C. Dixon the plantation
> on which I reside containing about fourteen hundred acres to them
> & their heirs forever, reserving however the right of my son, Thomas C.
> the first choice;
> I give to my son Thomas Cato West my two old negroes George
> & Peggy, my saddle horse, Prince, also my gold watch;
> I give to my daughter Martha C. Dixon my old Negro woman
> Amonet, also my Buggy and horse John;
> I give to my son Thomas Cato & Martha C. Dixon all of my
> Household & Kitchen furniture, also all of my stock of every descrip-
> tion, also all of my farming utensils, they Thomas Cato & Martha
> C. Dixon paying to my grand children the sum of fourteen hundred
> Dollars to be divided into three equal parts, one part to Kate West
> & Charles children of Thomas Reed, one part to Charles West &
> Jane Davidson children of J. H. Dorsey, and the remaining one part
> to Charles Hunter, son of my son Charles W. West.
> I give to my two Grand Children Kate West & Charles children
> of Thomas Reed, in lieu of any land, the following negroes [now in the?]
> possession of their Father, for their use, to wit, Milly, [Julien?]
> child, to them and their heirs forever.
> I give to my two Grand Children Charles West & Jane Davidson,
> children of J. H. Dorsey, in lieu of any land, the following Negroes, to wit,

[260] *Southern Telegraph* (Rodney, Miss.), 5 September 1838, v.1, no.17, p.3, col.2, obituary of Charlotte West.
[261] 1850 U.S. census, Jefferson Co., Miss., Fayette, p.100 stamped, p.199 written, dwelling and family 276; NARA microfilm M432, roll 374. 1860 U.S. census, Jefferson Co., Miss., Police Dist. 3, p.36, dwelling 283, family 294; NARA microfilm M653, roll 584.
[262] Jefferson Co., Miss., Marriage Records, Book B:253; FHL microfilm 893,070.
[263] Brown, *Jefferson Co, Miss., Cemeteries, Etc.,* 2:99.
[264] Viz., "Kate" (Hunter) West, Charles H. West, and [Charles] West Dorsey.

Olwell and little Sally and her child, to them & their heirs forevers.
I give to my Grand Son Charles Hunter, child of my son
Charles William West, in lieu of any land, the following Negroes, to wit,
Leroy & his wife Sally & her child Emaline, to him and his heirs forever.
I give to my niece Laura West, daughter of my brother Richard
Claiborne West, Fifteen Hundred Dollars, to be paid to her by my
Executor as soon after my death as convenient.
The plantation on which my son Thomas C. now resides
called the Mount Nebo place I desire sold by my Executor on a credit
of one, two, & three years, and the proceeds divided into three Equal
parts, one part thereof I give to my grand children Kate West &
Charles children of Thomas Reed, one part to my grand children
Charles West & Jane Davidson, children of J. H. Dorsey, and the
remaining one part to my grand son Charles Hunter child of
my son Charles W. West, to them and their heirs forever,
The rest, residue, and remainder of my estate real and per
sonal, shall be divided into five equal parts in value by com
missioners, to be appointed by the Probate Court of Jefferson County,
one part thereof I give to my son Thomas Cato, one part to my
daughter Martha C. Dixon, one part to my two grand children
Kate West & Charles, children of Thomas Reed, one part to my two
grand children Charles West & Jane David[son] children of J. H.
Dorsey, and the remaining one part to my grand son Charles
Hunter, child of my son Charles William West, and in such
division, the Negroes, which my children or grand children
or their parents may have in their possession, for the use of my
grand children, at the time of my death, may be returned by
such child of [sic: or?] grandchild, as so much of its portion at the valu-
ation to be fixed by said Commissioners.
I appoint my son Thomas Cato West my Executor of this
my last will and Testament, no bond or security required from
my Executor.
In testimony whereof, I have hereunto set my hand
this 19th day of April 1859 in my own hand writing.

Charles West [signature] {seal}

Exhibit B
Codicil, to my last will and Testament dated 19th of April
A.D. 1859, made this 22nd day of August A.D. 1859.
Item, I will & direct that all my Estate, both real & personal
that may descent to & be inherited by or descend to my grand children
Charles West & Jane Davidson, children of my late daughter
Jane Dorsey be held in trust, controled [sic] & managed by my son
Thomas Cato West during the minority of them my said grand children

or until the said Jane Davidson marries, and that my said son
Thomas C. West shall maintain & Educate my said grand children
out of the proceeds of said property.
And further, should my said grand children Charles West
and Jane Davidson, children of my late daughter Jane Dorsey
die without issue, then I will & direct that all of the Estate
devised by me to them, or inherited by them, from me shall

revert to & descend to my surviving children and my grand
children and their descendants, share and share alike.
In Witness whereof I have hereunto set my hand &
seal this 22nd day of August A.D. 1859, in my own hand writing.
Charles West [signature] {seal}[265]

Charles West died on 22 October 1861, according to his son's petition to probate the will.[266] The chancery packet D-182 for his estate is missing from the FHL microfilm and from the courthouse. Although Charles's will identifies nine slaves by name, the 1860 slave schedule shows he then held 51 slaves in all and 18 slave houses.[267] No separate recording of his inventory has been found. His final resting place has not been located.

The children of Charles[4] West and Charlotte E. Neely:

    i.   (UNKNOWN FEMALE)[5] WEST, born 1822-1826,[268] died before 1838.[269]

    ii.   FRANCES JANE[5] WEST, b. 20 March 1828; married John H. Dorsey;[270] died 15 February 1854.[271] Children: *(a)* Charles West, ca.1851-aft.1870[272]; *(b)* Jane Davidson, ca.1854-aft.1870.[273]

    iii.   CHARLES WILLIAM WEST, b. 16 April 1830; married Catherine "Kate" Hunter;[274] died 31 March 1859.[275] Children: *(a)* Susan Charlotte, 3 October 1853-

---

[265] Jefferson Co., Miss., Will Book B:61-63; will of Charles West, 19 April 1859, codicil dated 22 August 1859, proved 2 December 1861; FHL microfilm 893,068.

[266] Ibid., B:60, son's probate petition.

[267] 1860 U.S. census, Jefferson Co., Miss., slave schedule, Police Dist. No. 3, p.86-87 (written) and p.99-100 (stamped), Charles West owner or manager; NARA microfilm M653, roll 599.

[268] *Mississippi Free Trader* (Natchez., Miss.), 1 May 1850, v.15, no.37, p.2, col.1: "Married—At Cherokee Bower, on the 11th instant, by the Rev. J. H. Davidson, of Louisiana, Dr. John H. Dorsey, to Miss Francis [*sic*] Jane, second daughter of Charles West, Esq., of Jefferson County." The identity of Charles's first daughter is unknown.

[269] *Southern Telegraph* (Rodney, Miss.), 5 September 1838, v.1, no.17, p.3, col.2, obituary of Charlotte West: "She has, no doubt, joined her *first* and last *born*, two lovely babes, that had gone before her" [emphasis added].

[270] *Mississippi Free Trader* (Natchez., Miss.), 1 May 1850, v.15, no.37, p.2, col.1, Dorsey-West marriage notice.

[271] *Find a Grave* (www.findagrave.com), Frances Jane West, wife of J. H. Dorsey, 15 February 1854, memorial 23782216, by "NatalieMaynor"; photograph (Fayette Cemetery, Jefferson Co., Miss.). Born 20 March 1828.

[272] 1860 U.S. census, Jefferson Co., Miss., Police Dist. 3, p.36, dwelling 283, family 294, (grandfather) Charles West's household includes West Dorsey, age nine; NARA microfilm M653, roll 584. 1870 U.S. census, Jefferson Co., Miss., Township No. 9, p.39 written, p.82 stamped, dwelling 313, family 312, T. C. West household includes West Dorsey, age eighteen; NARA microfilm M593, roll 733.

[273] 1860 U.S. census, Jefferson Co., Miss., Police Dist. 3, p.36 written, dwelling 289, family 279, household of William J. Gibson (spouse of Jane's great-aunt Catherine (Neely) Elam Gibson) includes Jane Dorsey, age seven; NARA microfilm M653, roll 584. 1870 U.S. census, Jefferson Co., Miss., Township No. 9, p.39 written, p.82 stamped, dwelling 313, family 312, T. C. West household includes Jinnie Dorsey, age sixteen; NARA microfilm M593, roll 733.

[274] Claiborne Co., Miss., Marriage Records, 1849-1869, vol.6-7, West-Hunter, 9 December 1852; FHL microfilm 875,443.

[275] *Find a Grave* (www.findagrave.com), Charles W. West, 31 March 1859, memorial 11516022, by "NatalieMaynor"; photograph (Fayette Cemetery, Jefferson Co., Miss.). Born 16 April 1820. Brown, *Jefferson Co., Miss., Cemeteries, Etc.*, 2:98. This publication gives death date inscription as 31 March "1853," but the tombstone photograph shows "1859." Also, the 1859 will of Charles West and the 1860 U.S. census entry of the elder Charles West with his daughter-in-law and young Charles Hunter West indicate that the death year had to be 1858 or 1859.

6 February 1857[276]; *(b)* Mattie Anne, 25 February 1856-3 November 1858[277]; *(c)* Charles Hunter, b.ca.1858-d.8 June 1933.[278]

iv.   THOMAS CATO WEST, b.ca. 1831; married Martha "Patsy" Forman; died 11 April 1872. Children: *(a)* Howell Forman, 28 March 1853-14 February 1914[279]; *(b)* Emma J., 7 April 1856-8 November 1926[280]; *(c)* Thomas C., 1861-1920.[281]

v.   LAVENIA W. WEST, b. ca. 1835; married Thomas Reed;[282] d. 4 April 1851.[283] Children: *(a)* Kate West, b.ca.1848-d.14 July 1864[284]; *(b)* Charles West, 24 January 1851-28 February 1896.[285]

vi.   MARTHA C. WEST, b. ca. 1837; married Minor C. Dixon;[286] died after 29 July 1885.[287] Children: *(a)* Henry/Harvy, ca.1857[288]; *(b)* Minor Jennings, 2 November 1858-17 September 1895[289]; *(c)* Lorena "Gabrie E.," b.ca.1864[290] ; *(d)* Susan B., b.ca.1866[291]; *(e)* Mattie M., ca.1869-25 September 1895.[292]

---

[276] Brown, *Jefferson Co., Miss., Cemeteries, Etc.*, 2:99, Fayette Cemetery, "Dau. of C.W. & K West."

[277] Ibid.

[278] *Find a Grave* (www.findagrave.com), Charles Hunter West, 1858-1933, memorial 55766028 by "M. G. Slade"; photograph (Greenville Cemetery, Washington Co., Miss.).

[279] *Find a Grave* (www.findagrave.com), Howell Forman West, 1853-1914, memorial 43361136 by Michelle Woodham; photograph (Natchez City Cemetery, Natchez, Miss.).

[280] *Find a Grave* (www.findagrave.com), Emma Jane West, 6 April 1856-8 November 1926, memorial 43361048 by Michelle Woodham; photograph (Natchez City Cemetery, Natchez, Miss.).

[281] *Find a Grave* (www.findagrave.com), Thomas Claiborne West, 1861-1920, memorial 118344795 by Ruby Carman; photograph (Natchez City Cemetery, Natchez, Miss.). *Natchez Democrat* (Natchez, Miss.), 29 January 1920, v.54, no.127, p.5, col.6, death notice.

[282] *Mississippi Free Trader* (Natchez., Miss.), 22 December 1847, v.13, no.19, p.3, col.2: "Married—By the Rev. B. M. Drake on Thursday, the 9th inst., Thomas Reed, Esq., of Natchez, Miss., to Miss Lavinia W. West, at the residence of her father Chas. West, Esq., in Jefferson county, Miss."

[283] Brown, *Jefferson Co., Miss., Cemeteries, Etc.*, vol. 2:98. Age sixteen at death.

[284] Brown, *Jefferson Co., Miss., Cemeteries, Etc.*, vol. 2:99, Fayette Cemetery, "Died at age 16 years, Dau. of Thos. Reed."

[285] *Find a Grave* (www.findgrave.com), Charles W. Reed, 24 January 1851-28 February 1896, memorial 104881773 by Ruby Carman; photograph (Natchez City Cemetery, Natchez, Miss.).

[286] Jefferson Co., Miss., Marriages, Bk B:310, Dixon-West, 29 June 1856; FHL microfilm 893,070. "Martha West & Minor Dixon were married Sunday morning [29 June] by Mr. French. They will take a trip to Madison County to visit Minor's relations"; Darden Diary transcription (https://jeffersoncountyms.org/darden1856.htm), 1 July 1856 entry; transcribed from the Susan (Sillers) Darden, Diary (Jefferson Co., Miss., 9 June 1853–31 December 1861), vol. 1, unpaginated; Darden Family Papers (Z/0082.000), MDAH microfilm roll 35992; Mississippi State Archives, Jackson.

[287] On this date, Mrs. Martha C. Dixon was named as a contingent beneficiary in her aunt Catherine (Neely) Elam Gibson's will. Jefferson Co., Miss., Will Book B:169, Catherine N. Gibson, 29 July 1885; FHL microfilm 893,068; Chancery Court, probate packet D-468, Catherine N. Gibson; FHL microfilm 1,905,641.

[288] 1860 U.S. census, Jefferson Co., Miss., Fayette, p.1 and p.583 written, dwelling and family 1, Minor C. Dixon household, "Harvy" age 3; NARA microfilm M653, roll 584.

[289] *Helena Weekly World* (Helena, Ark.), 15 September 1895, v.24, no.43, p.3, col.2; obituary of Dr. M.J. Dixon.

[290] 1870 U.S. census, Jefferson Co., Miss., Twp. 9, p.95 stamped, 65 written, dwelling 574, family 573, M.C. Dixon household, Lorena 6; NARA microfilm M593, roll 733. 1880 U.S. census, Jefferson Co., Miss., Fayette, ED62, p.208 stamped, p.11 written, dwelling 117, family 106, Martha C. Dixon household, Gabrie E. age 16; NARA microfilm T9, roll 651.

[291] Ibid., Susan age 14.

[292] Ibid., Mattie age 10. Also *Helena Weekly World* (Helena, Ark.), 25 September 1895, v.24, no.44, p.3, col.7; obituary of Mrs. T. Elbert Bonner, sister of the late M.J. Dixon.

vii.   (UNKNOWN CHILD) WEST, born ca. 1838.[293]

11. SUSAN[4] WEST (*Cato[3], William[2,1]*), daughter of Cato West and Martha Wills Green,[294] was born before 1792 in the Natchez District.[295] No records contemporary to Susan's lifetime have been located in which she appeared by name; however, the Green family Bible includes her as one of Cato West and Martha Wills Green's children, noting that she "married THOMAS WEST, her cousin."[296] Susan may have married around 1810, at age eighteen. If Susan indeed married her first cousin Thomas W. West (son of Charles West and Sarah Withers),[297] then she does not appear to be living by 1816, when "T. W. West" appeared in the territorial census of Jefferson County as the only white individual in his household.[298]

Thomas W. West next married Mary Chinn in Wilkinson County, Miss., on 3 February 1818.[299] Although Thomas had children by his second wife, his first child—Martha Octavia—appears to be by his first wife. Martha Octavia's age in 1830 (fifteen to twenty, born 1810-1815), 1850 (thirty-five; born 1815) and 1860 (forty-four, born 1816) place her birth before Thomas's second marriage, as does her reported age at her death in November 1867 (fifty-three, born about 1814).[300]

The likely child of Susan[4] West and Thomas W. West:

---

[293] *Southern Telegraph* (Rodney, Miss.), 5 September 1838, v.1, no.17, p.3, col.2, obituary of Charlotte West: "She has, no doubt, joined her first and *last born*, two lovely babes, that had gone before her" [emphasis added].

[294] Green family Bible transcription in supporting documentation for NSDAR nat. no. 373,979, 13.

[295] Assumes she is one of the three girls who, along with three boys, were enumerated in Cato West's household in the 1792 territorial census of Villa Gayoso (later Jefferson County).

[296] Green family Bible transcription in supporting documentation for NSDAR nat. no. 373,979, 13. This same information appears in Clay and Ewing genealogies, which do not mirror other information in (and thus not copied from) the Green family Bible; Zachary F. Smith and Mrs. Mary Rogers Clay, *The Clay Family* (Louisville, Ky.: John P. Morton & Co., 1899), 224. Presley Kittredge Ewing and Mary Ellen (Williams) Ewing, *The Ewing Genealogy with Cognate Branches* (Houston, Tex.: by the compilers, 1919), 134-140.

[297] Fauquier Co., Va., "Marriage Bonds and Returns, No. 1, 1759-1800," 143, Charles West and "Sally" Withers, 10 June 1785, typed transcript of bond and father's consent for "Salley" but no return; FHL microfilm 31,633. *FamilySearch* (www.familysearch.org), "Original Spanish Record, 1781-1796," Spanish records, vol. 31-32 1795, vol. 32:322-335, original "testimento de Dr. Carlos West," 1 September 1795, proved 17 September 1795; FHL microfilm 893,509.

[298] *FamilySearch* (www.familysearch.org), "Mississippi territorial census: RG 2, series 497, 1801-1816," digital images, Territorial census, Box 17981, Jefferson County, 1816, digital film 4822295, 15th page, image 136, T. W. West; citing MDAH, Jackson, Mississippi: one male over twenty-one (on the same sheet with Cato's son "Thos. West"; the male under age twenty-one in the latter's household is likely the orphaned John Ewing mentioned in Thomas's 1818 will). Presumably any infant daughter of the widowed Thomas was cared for by her West relatives in a different household.

[299] Wilkinson Co., Miss., Marriages A:28 bond; B:103-104 return, West-Chinn, both records signed on 3 February 1818; FHL microfilm 877,597.

[300] 1830 U.S. census, Wilkinson Co., Miss., p.247 stamped and written; NARA microfilm M19, roll 71. Thos. W. West is fifth name from bottom, female age fifteen to twenty fits. 1840 U.S. census, West Feliciana Par., La., p.208 stamped; NARA microfilm M704, roll 130. Lewis Davis is fifth name from bottom, only female in household is age twenty to thirty; the next entry is for Octavia's stepmother "Mrs. Mary [Chinn] West." 1850 U.S. census, West Feliciana Parish, La., p.272B stamped, 544 written, dwelling 335, family 340; NARA microfilm M432, roll 231. Robert Malloy household with Octavia Malloy, age thirty-five. *Weekly Gazette and Comet* (Baton Rouge, La.), Saturday, 9 November 1867, v.49, no.45, p.3, col 2: "Died: In this city, on Saturday, the 2d inst., of yellow fever, Mrs. Octavia Molloy, aged 53 years, a native of Jefferson County, Miss...."

Perhaps i.   MARTHA OCTAVIA[5] WEST, b.ca.1815[301]; married (1) Lewis H. Davis, 2 June 1833, Wilkinson Co., Miss.[302] Children: *(a)* Robert Thomas, b.ca.1834-aft.1850[303]; *(b)* Hugh Howard, b.ca.1839-aft.1850[304]; and *(c)* Lewis Henry, b.aft.1839-d.bef.1850?[305]; married (2) Robert Malloy, 1 August 1850, West Feliciana Parish, La.[306]; child: Ella Octavia, b.ca.1851.

12. ANN[4] WEST (*Cato[3], William[2,1]*), daughter of Cato West and Martha Wills Green,[307] was born in the Natchez District about 1794, according to her age as reported in a published obituary.[308] In 1846, Ann stated that she first married in 1811 to JOSEPH WINN; the location was probably Jefferson County, Mississippi Territory, although theirs was not among the extant marriage records.[309] Their marriage definitely occurred after May 1809, at which time Joseph Winn, Obadiah Kirkland, and Joseph Woodward received a passport from the governor of Georgia to pass though the Creek Nation, making their way to the Mississippi Territory.[310]

---

[301] Ibid.

[302] Wilkinson Co., Miss., Marriages E:334, bond and license, Davis-West (Thos. C. West bondsman, T. Davidson also signed), 28 May 1833; solemnized by A. J. Randolph, Judge of Probates, on 2 June 1833; FHL microfilm 877,599. No consents recorded although both underage.

[303] 1850 U.S. census, West Feliciana Parish, La., p.272B stamped, p.544 written, dwelling 335, family 340, Robert Malloy household with (stepson) Robert T. Davis, age sixteen; NARA microfilm M432, roll 231.

[304] Ibid; (stepson) Hugh H., age eleven.

[305] West Feliciana Parish, La., Probate Record, vol. 11 (1848-1851):72-74, 2 June 1848, administratrix Octavia M. Davis filed final account of administration of Lewis H. Davis estate no. 82. At his decease, Davis "left three minor children, viz: Robert Thomas, Hugh Howard, and Lewis Henry, who are his legal forced heirs..."; FHL microfilm 364,680. Youngest child Lewis Henry David not found in the family's 1850 household.

[306] West Feliciana Par., La., Marriage Record, vol. A:182-183, Robert Malloy and William T. West security bond and license to marry Mrs. Octavia M. Davis, 31 July 1850; solemnized on 1 August 1850 by W. Hamilton Watkins, an Elder in the Meth. Epis. Church, South, in presence of J. Hunter Collins, A. Wilson, and Bertrand Haralson; FHL microfilm 364,651.

[307] Green family Bible transcription in supporting documentation for NSDAR nat. no. 373,979, 13.

[308] *Nashville Christian Advocate*, 7 December 1849, v.14, no.6, whole no. 682, fourth page of unpaginated newspaper.

[309] "Judge James M. Ellis letter of 9 November 1872," The Draper Manuscript Collection, microfilm edition, 147 rolls (Chicago: Filmed by the University of Chicago, 197?), Series VV, Sumter MSS, vol. 13, document 124; FHL microfilm 889,218. Judge Ellis located the petition for dower that "Ann Deloach" filed in Franklin County on 14 May 1846. It stated she married Joseph Winn in 1811 and that in 1846 she was living in Holmes County. Green family Bible transcription in NSDAR nat. no. 373,979: "Ann married Joseph Winn."

[310] Dorothy Williams Potter, *Passports of Southeastern Pioneers, 1770-1823* (1982 reprint 1990 Gen. Publ. Co., Baltimore, Md.), 238, 25 May 1809, on recommendation of John Herbert Esq., passport through the Creek nation prepared for Joseph Woodward, Joseph Winn, and Obediah Kirkland; cited as appearing on p.446 of "Georgia Executive Proceedings, Feb 1808 - Nov 1809, drawer 50, roll 46."

Joseph Winn (son of John Winn and Penelope Kirkland)[311] served as sheriff of adjacent Franklin County, M.T., from 1812 to 1815,[312] and the family's 1816 territorial census entry there included one male and two females under age twenty-one.[313] Letters addressed to Joseph Winn arriving at the Washington, Adams County, post office on 1 January 1819 were still uncollected by 27 January 1819.[314] In 1820, the family appeared in both the federal and state censuses in Franklin County, with Joseph's mother Penelope listed immediately after them in the state census.[315] Joseph Winn served as state representative from Franklin County in this year.[316] On 12 October 1821, Joseph signed a receipt acknowledging payment from the estate of his late father-in-law Cato West for 400 bushels of corn.[317] Estate records for Ann's brother John S. West show that Joseph Winn purchased John's slave, Wat, prior to 25 April 1826.[318] An appeal of a court case in 1834 involved the 1819 debt of the then-former firm of Joseph Winn and Charles C. Slocumb, both the names of men who represented Franklin County in the state legislature in the 1820s.[319]

Joseph Winn died sometime before 1830, when "Ann Winn" was enumerated back in her native Jefferson County.[320] Franklin County lost all its early records in an 1876 courthouse fire and no

---

[311] Rutherford County, Tennessee, Record Book 2:298-230, 8 December 1813 (recorded 2 November 1814), will of John Winn; FHL microfilm 380,487. Jefferson Co., Miss., Probate Record A-3:353, 30 December 1833, division of personal property of Mr. John Winn and wife Mrs. Penelope Winn (among seven children as specified in John's 1813 will); FHL microfilm 1,939,757. A modern transcription of an 1858 letter states that Penelope Kirkland was John Winn's second wife (Samuel Winn, 29 July 1858, letter sent from Henry County, Tenn., to Jabez Lamar Monroe Curry; transcription posted by Jon Blocker to *RootsWeb.com* on 26 March 2008; (https://lists.rootsweb.com/ hyperkitty/list/winn.rootsweb.com/thread/30452578/).

[312] "Commission, Acting Governor Daingerfield, Washington, appointing Joseph Winn as Sheriff of Franklin County," 28 March 1812 took oath, 8 July 1815 resigned; MDAH, image, (http://mdah.state.ms.us/arrec/ digital_archives/series/s488/detail/9406); document no. 1362, Administration of Acting Governor Henry Daingerfield; MDAH Series 488 "Administration Papers, 1769, 1788-1817; n.d."

[313] *FamilySearch* (www.familysearch.org), "Mississippi territorial census: RG 2, series 497, 1801-1816," digital images, Territorial census, Box 17014, Franklin County, 1816, digital film 4822294, 5th page, image 48, Joseph Winn; citing MDAH, Jackson, Mississippi: 2 males over age twenty-one (b.bef.1795), one male under twenty-one (b.aft.1795), 2 females over twenty-one, 2 females under twenty-one, 10 slaves, 17 total.

[314] *Mississippi State Gazette* (Natchez, Miss.), 27 January 1819, v.7, letters remaining at the Washington post office since 1 January 1819; "Mississippi 19th and 20th Newspapers in Original Format," Library of Congress control no. 8568.

[315] 1820 U.S. census, Franklin Co., Miss., p.40, entry 17; NARA microfilm M33, roll 57. Note: at the time of this publication, *Ancestry.com* indexes this entry as Amite County although "Franklin" is written in the margin. *FamilySearch* (www.familysearch.org), "Mississippi, State and Territorial Collection, 1792-1866," digital images, 1820, Franklin County, image 5, Joseph Winn (25th entry) and Penny Winn (26th entry); citing Heritage Quest, microfilm V229. 3 rolls.

[316] Robert Lowry and William H. McCardle, *A History of Mississippi: from the Discovery of the Great River by Hernando DeSoto, Including the Earliest Settlement Made by the French Under Iberville, to the Death of Jefferson Davis (1541-1889)* (Jackson, Miss.: R. H. Henry & Co., 1891), 477; sketch of Franklin County lists the state representatives: 1820 Representative Joseph Winn.

[317] Jefferson Co., Miss., Chancery Court, probate packet B-98, Cato West Jr. [*sic*]; FHL microfilm 1,889,020.

[318] Jefferson Co., Miss., Chancery Court, probate packet B-99, John S. West; FHL microfilm 1,889,020.

[319] Volney E. Howard, "Slocumb's Administrator, Appellant, v. Holmes's Administrator," July Term 1834, *Reports of Cases Argued and Determined in the High Court of Errors and Appeals of the State of Mississippi* (Philadelphia: T. K. & P G. Collings, 1839), 139. Lowry and McCardle, *A History of Mississippi* (1891), 477; 1825 Representative "C. C. Slocum"; 1826 Senator Charles C. Slocumb.

[320] 1830 U.S. census, Jefferson Co., Miss., p.39, line 13; NARA microfilm M19, roll 71; Ann Winn 30-40 (b.1790-1800), 2 males twenty to thirty (1800-1810), 2 males ten to fifteen (1815-1820), 1 female fifteen to twenty (1810-

probate records have been located for Joseph Winn's estate.[321] Ann apparently moved her family north by 1832 when Ann Winn, brother R[ichard]. C[laiborne]. West, and nephew J[ames]. R[aiford]. West first appeared on a Yazoo County, Miss., tax list.[322] On 27 January 1834 she was recorded as a resident of Holmes County—newly formed from Yazoo County—when she purchased just over 120 acres of public land there.[323] On 23 December 1834, she purchased 80 more acres.[324] A deed recorded less than two years later shows that she next married ELIAS F. DELOACH before 19 November 1836, on which date they sold her first-purchased tract to her former sister-in-law Sarah (Kirkland) West Parker.[325]

Two individuals provided information about Ann (West) Winn Deloach to Lyman Copeland Draper when he solicited testimony from early settlers of land west of the Allegheny Mountains. First, "Mr. A. ___," of Port Gibson, Claiborne County, Mississippi, relayed information he learned from John M. Pintard, a carpenter in Jefferson County.[326] Pintard recalled that Joseph Winn's widow Ann West remarried to a Mr. Deloach and settled near Lexington (Holmes County), Mississippi.[327] Second, Jefferson County Chancery Judge James M. Ellis sent the following account to Draper:

> Fayette, Jeff. Co., Miss., Nov. 9th, 1872
> Lyman C. Draper, Esquire
> Dear Sir,
> ...At my recent Term of Chancery Court in Franklin County I made a search and find that one Joseph Winn was Sheriff of that Co. in 1814—I understood he came from South Carolina. I also found a petition for dower filed by Ann Deloach as widow of Joseph Winn deceased in certain real estate in Franklin Co. Filed May 14-1846—she was then

---

1815), 1 female ten to fifteen (1815-1820), 2 females five to ten (1820-1825). Ann's mother-in-law is likely the one represented on a different census page for Jefferson County as "Mrs. P. Winn" (p.41, line 7; female age fifty to sixty, b.1770-1780).

[321] James M. White and Franklin Lafayette Riley, "Section 2: County Offices," *Publications of the Mississippi Historical Society* (Oxford, Miss.: for the Society, 1902), 5:137.

[322] *FamilySearch* (www.familysearch.org), "Mississippi, State Archives, Various Records, 1820-1951; Yazoo, County tax rolls, 1823-1832, Box 3800," digital images, digital film 4854376, image 353, no page number, 1832 combined assessment, "J.R. & R.C. West" (seventh entry on page) and "Ann Winn" (tenth entry on page).

[323] Ann Winn (Holmes County), cash entry file, certificate no. 16577, 27 January 1834, $50.45, 40.36 acres, S½, E½, SE¼, Sec. 30, Township 14, Range 1 East, Mt. Salus, Mississippi, Land Office; Land Entry Papers, 1800-1908; Records of the Bureau of Land Management, Record Group 49; National Archives, Washington DC. Ann Winn, cash entry file, certificate 16580, 27 January 1834, $100, 80 acres W½, SE¼, Sec. 20, T14N, R1E.

[324] Ann Winn, cash entry file, certificate no. 19171, 23 December 1834, $99.99, 79.99 acres: E½, SE¼, Sec. 30, T14N, R1E. This file includes a sworn statement signed by Samuel Atchison (her son-in-law), dated 8 December 1834, that he inspected the property and found no one residing thereon or "an circumtrix [? handwriting is very bad] the same except Ann Winn the person for whose benefit this affidavit is made..."; sent to Mrs. Ann Winn, Rankin P. Office, Mississippi.

[325] Holmes Co., Miss., Deed Book A:395, Elias F. Deloach and Anne his wife to Sarah Parker, 19 November 1836; FHL microfilm 879,459. For $300 they sold the SE¼ ("S½ of the E½") of the SE¼ of Sec 30, T14N, R1E, 40 and 36/100 acres. The Deloaches both signed and acknowledged the sale on the same date; no witnesses.

[326] Pintard made the coffin for Ann's brother-in-law John A. Davidson in 1823 (Jefferson Co., Miss., Chancery Court, probate packet B-182, FHL microfilm 1,901,538).

[327] "T. G. Jones letter of 29 May 1873," The Draper Manuscript Collection, microfilm edition, 147 rolls (Chicago: Filmed by the University of Chicago, 197?), Series VV, Sumter MSS, vol. 13, document 115a; FHL microfilm 889,218.

residing in Holmes Co., Miss. The petition states she was married to said Joseph Winn in the year 1811.[328]

In 1839, the Deloaches resided at the tavern house on lots 26 and 27 in Lexington, Holmes County, but they were not enumerated there in the 1840 federal census.[329] The 1841 state census enumerated them in Bolivar County, Mississippi, northwest of Holmes County.[330] Elias F. Deloach, born 1781-1791,[331] died in Bolivar County prior to April 1843.[332] Following the death of her second husband, Ann returned to Holmes County. An 1845 personal tax roll there appears to record her neighbor or overseer, Josiah Dunn, whose residence is noted as "A. Deloach's near Emery."[333]

A Methodist newspaper noted the passing of Ann (West) Winn Deloach in Holmes County:

> Departed this life, on the 5th of September, 1849, at the residence of Mrs. S. Parker [her former sister-in-law], in Holmes county, Miss., sister Ann Deloach; aged 55 years.
> The deceased embraced our holy religion and joined the Methodist Church in the year 1831; was faithful unto death; left the world of her pilgrimage glorifying in the cross of Christ, triumphing in the blissful hope of immortality beyond the grave, and exhorting her relatives and friends to meet her in heaven. "So Mote it be." Jas. A. Godfrey. Black Hawk, Miss., Oct. 23, 1849.[334]

The Salem Church cemetery near Tolarsville, Holmes County, borders part of the property Ann (West) Winn Deloach purchased in the early 1830s, and part of a surviving tombstone there was transcribed in the 1950s as "Ann E."[335] This tombstone likely does not belong to "Ann H."

---

[328] "Judge James M. Ellis letter of 9 November 1872," The Draper Manuscript Collection, Series VV, Sumter MSS, vol. 13, document 124; FHL microfilm 889,218. The original petition does not survive in Franklin County, per Lynn Perry, Deputy Clerk, 24 February 2010 email to author. 1870 U.S. census, Jefferson Co., Miss., Twp. 9, P. O. Fayette, p.74 stamped, p.23 written, dwelling 186, family 185, James M. Ellis; NARA microfilm M593, roll 733; occupation "Chancery Judge."

[329] "Sheriff's Sale," *Lexington Union* (Lexington, Miss.), 6 April 1839, v.1, no.21, p.4, col.5.

[330] *FamilySearch* (http://familysearch.org) "Mississippi, State Archives, Various Records, 1820-1951; Bolivar [Co.], State census returns 1841, Box 10449," digital film 4827034, image 82, 1841, p.2, 14th name on page, Deloach, Elias F., 1 male age five to ten, 1 male ten to fifteen, 1 male fifty to sixty; 1 female five to ten, 1 female fifteen to twenty, 1 female forty to fifty.

[331] Ibid.; eldest male age fifty to sixty in 1841

[332] Deloach's Bolivar County, Miss., Chancery Court probate packet no. 23 is missing, but a transcription of Bolivar County Docket Book I:12 shows Joseph McGuire obtained letters of administration on Deloach's estate at the April 1843 court (Katherine C. Branton and Alice C. Wade, *Early Mississippi Records, Bolivar County, Vol. 1 (1836-1861)* (N.pl.: 1988), 7).

[333] *FamilySearch* (www.familysearch.org), "Mississippi, State Archives, Various Records, 1820-1951; Holmes, County tax rolls 1833-1846, Box 3658," digital film 4845439, image 282, Personal [Tax] Roll, 1845, p.13, 13th name on page, Josiah Dunn.

[334] *Nashville Christian Advocate*, 7 December 1849, v.14, no.6, whole no. 682, fourth page of unpaginated newspaper. The author Godfrey (b.ca.1820 S.C.) was enumerated as a Methodist minister in 1850 in Carroll County, Miss., and in 1870 in Amite County, Miss. No entry was found for Ann Deloach in the 1850 mortality schedule for Holmes County.

[335] McNees, *Holmes County Cemetery Records* (1955), 120.

(West) Winn Deloach,[336] but nevertheless she likely was interred in this cemetery where tombstones identify many of her other kinsmen.[337]

The children of Ann[4] West and Joseph Winn:

Perhaps i.	(UNKNOWN FEMALE)[5] WINN, born about 1812; died after 1830.[338]	
Perhaps ii.	(UNKNOWN MALE) WINN, born about 1814; died after 1830.[339]	
iii.	MARTHA P. WINN, born about 1815; married Samuel Atchison before 11 March 1833 in Yazoo Co., Miss.;[340] died 15 August 1853, Carroll Co., Miss.: "Died— Near Black Hawk, Miss., on the 15th August, after a protracted illness, Mrs. Martha P. Atchison, wife of Samuel Atchison, Esq., and daughter of Joseph and Ann Winn, aged 39 years. In early life she dedicated herself to God, and connected herself with the Church, and was a faithful member. 'Blessed are the dead that die in the Lord. The bright and joyful testimony she left behind, gives us abundant assurance that our loss is her eternal gain.'"[341] Children: *(a)* Sarah Ann, b.ca.1834[342]; *(b)* James, b.ca.1836[343]; and *(c)* Elizabeth Jane, b.ca.1838.[344]	
Perhaps iv.	(UNKNOWN FEMALE) WINN, born about 1818; died after 1820.[345]	
v.	Susannah Augusta Winn, born about 1825 in Miss., married Richard Sparks Phillips, born about 1808 in Miss.[346] Children: *(a)* Oliver Winn, 27 February	

---

[336] Middle initial of "H." appears in her deed with second husband E. F. Deloach dated 2 December 1836, Holmes Co., Miss., Deed Book A:395. She may have been named "Ann Harwood," after her aunt Ann Harwood Green (Green family Bible transcription in supporting documentation for NSDAR nat. no. 373,979).

[337] By 1849, the relatives of Ann's who are known to be interred in the Salem Cemetery included William E. Parker (second husband of her former sister-in-law Sarah (Kirkland) West Parker) and three children of her nephew James Raiford West.

[338] 1830 U.S. census, Jefferson Co., Miss., 39 stamped, 207 written, 13th name, Ann Winn household, one female age fifteen to twenty; NARA microfilm M19, roll 71.

[339] 1830 U.S. census, Jefferson Co., Miss., 39 stamped, 207 written, 13th name, Ann Winn household, one male age fifteen to twenty; NARA microfilm M19, roll 71.

[340] Silas Emmett Lucas, *Marriages from Early Tennessee Newspapers*, 1794-1851 (Easley, S.C.: Southern Historical Press, 1978), 16 and 526; citing the Tennessee State Library and Archives' card file of marriage data from the *National Banner and Nashville Daily Advertiser*, 11 March 1833, Samuel Atchison, Esq., "married in Yazoo Co., Miss., to Miss Martha J. Winn."

[341] *New Orleans Christian Advocate* (New Orleans, La.), 10 September 1853, v.3, no.32, p.3, col.2.

[342] 1850 U.S. census, Carroll County, Miss., p.480 stamped, p.496 written, dwelling 630, family 694; NARA microfilm M432, roll 369.

[343] Ibid.

[344] Ibid.

[345] 1820 U.S. census, Franklin Co., Miss., p.40, entry 17, Joseph Winn household, female under age ten; NARA microfilm M33, roll 57.

[346] 1850 U.S. census, Holmes Co., Miss., p.292B stamped, p.584 written, dwelling and family 969, 9 October; Rich'd. S. Phillips household; NARA microfilm M432, roll 373. Full dates for Susannah's birth (4 June 1820), marriage to Richard Sparks Phillips (10 January 1841), and death (9 March 1856) are found on a sheet of paper, without source citation, in the supporting documentation for the NSDAR application of Hattie Phillips Callahan (national no. 340,698) on John Medearis (1744-1834, North Carolina), approved October 1943; National Society, Daughters of the American Revolution (NSDAR), Washington, D.C. William H. Norwood's *Genealogy of the Yancey-Medearis and Related Lines* (Corsicana, Tex.: Blackford Printing Co., 1958), 202-203, includes the same unsourced marriage date.

1849-3 May 1934,[347] *(b)* Benjamin West, 16 September 1852-15 May 1882[348] *(c)* Bettie, b.ca.1854, d.1864.[349]

vi.   AUGUSTUS O. WINN, born 8 September 1821; married Ann J. Pate on 27 August 1850 in Carroll Co., Miss.;[350] died 4 May 1858, Carroll Co., Miss.[351]

Perhaps vii.   (UNKNOWN FEMALE) WINN, born about 1824; died after 1830.

13. JOHN SMITH[4] WEST (*Cato[3], William[2,1]*), son of Cato West and Martha Wills Green,[352] was born in the Mississippi Territory after 1797, as Cato West's 1818 will names John as the first of his six youngest children then under age twenty-one.[353] He likely was named for Cato's stepfather John Smith, with whom Cato would have lived until reaching his majority and moving to South Carolina.

"John S. West" of "Mississippi" matriculated at the medical school of the University of Pennsylvania in Philadelphia in 1818-1819,[354] one of 422 such matriculates.[355] To be admitted, pupils living more than five miles from Philadelphia "must have studied with some reputable

---

[347] 1850 U.S. census, Holmes Co., Miss., p.292B; 1860 U.S. census, Holmes Co., Miss., Eulogy Beat, p.849, dwelling and family 991; NARA microfilm M653, roll 582. 1870 U.S. census, Holmes Co., Miss., Tchula Dist., p.200 stamped, p.15 written, dwelling 137, family 198; NARA microfilm M593, roll 731. 1880 U.S. census, Holmes Co., Miss., Beat 4, ED 8, p.206B stamped, p.24 written, dwelling 190, family 205; NARA microfilm T9, roll 650.

[348] 1860 U.S. census, Holmes Co., Miss., Eulogy Beat, p.849, dwelling and family 991; 1870 U.S. census, Holmes Co., Miss., Eulogy Beat, p.76B stamped, p.28 written, dwelling 137, family 198 (NARA microfilm M593, roll 731); 1880 U.S. census, Holmes Co., Miss., Beat 4, ED8, p.206B stamped, 24 written, dwelling 190, family 204.

[349] 1860 U.S. census, Holmes Co., Miss., Eulogy Beat, p.849, dwelling and family 991, for birth date. McNees, *Holmes County Cemetery Records* (1955), 120, for death. Indirect evidence for her parentage.

[350] Carroll County, Mississippi, Marriages vol. B, 32, Winn-Pate, 27 August 1850; FHL microfilm 895,136.

[351] Carroll Co., Miss., Will Record, 1st District, vol. A:162, A[ugustus]. O. Winn, 21 January 1858; FHL microfilm 895,115. *Find a Grave* (www.findagrave.com), Augustus O. Winn, 4 May 1858, memorial 41606832, by Beth Austin; photograph (Rose Hill Cemetery, Carroll Co., Miss.). Age at death calculates to the above birth date. Winn's 1858 will mentions that his wife Ann had not produced an heir, yet there is a 6-yr-old "Oliver Winn" in the widowed Ann's 1860 household; 1860 U.S. census, Carroll Co., Miss., 3rd Police District, p.15 written, dwelling 104, family 109; NARA microfilm M653, roll 578. A. O. Winn specified how his estate was to be distributed in the event Ann remained childless and transcriptions of the 1859 distribution records demonstrate that no heir had been born (http://valgenofindings. weebly.com/slavery-records.html#AugustusOWinn). The relationship of an "Oliver Winn" (b.ca.1854) to this Winn family is unresolved, but the census entry likely refers to A.O. Winn's *nephew* Oliver Winn *Phillips* (b.ca.1849), although the surname is missing and the age is wrong. The widow Ann (Pate) Winn served as guardian of the orphaned Oliver Winn Phillips's legacy from her late husband and that might explain his residence in her 1860 household (Carroll Co., Miss., "Probate Case Files, 165P-193P, 1858-1859"; File 186P, 1859, O.W. Phillips by Ann J. Winn, Gdn.; FHL microfilm 2,364,009).

[352] Jefferson County, Miss., Will Book A:24-25, will of Cato West, names "John Smith" West as one of his six youngest children. Also, Jefferson Co., Miss., Chancery Court, probate packet B-98, estate of Cato West, contains a 10 February 1819 letter from John S. West in Philadelphia (Pennsylvania) addressing Mr. Charles West as "Dear Brother."

[353] Jefferson Co., Miss., Will Book A:24-25, will of Cato West, 30 July 1818.

[354] Matriculates for 1818-19, "[School of Medicine] Matriculation Book commenced 1816 ended 1834," document no. 1576, p.33, Archives General Collection, Pre-1820, UPA 3, University Archives and Records Center, University of Pennsylvania. Entry no. 235: "John S. West, Mississippi."

[355] Joseph Carson, *A History of the Medical Department of the University of Pennsylvania: From its Foundation in 1765* (Philadelphia: Lindsay & Blakiston, 1869), 219. Of the 422, 102 graduated.

physician there for at least two years," according to rules the trustees passed in 1789, signed by Benjamin Franklin.[356]

During that first semester, John's brother Thomas West died, and his father died a few months later. "John S. West," presumably this one, had two letters waiting to be picked up at the Philadelphia post office on 16 January 1819, and "John Smith West" had two letters waiting on 31 July 1819.[357] A letter for "Dr. John West" waited on 28 February 1819.[358] The last newspaper notice of a letter waiting for "John West" was published on 20 September 1819.[359] The January letters possibly brought news of his father Cato's death. A surviving letter John wrote the next month illustrates his efforts to arrange his finances with the help of his brother Charles, who served as one of Cato's executors:

> Philadelphia, February 10[?]th, 1819
> Mr. Charles West
> Dear Brother, I have written a few days
> since, advising my intention of [Drawing?] on you in a
> few days. I have now negotiated a draft on you
> at twenty days [s?]ight for Two hundred dollars in
> favor of Mr. John H. Robinson which I hope
> will be honor'd on receipt -- I remain dear Brother
> affectionately yours,
> Jno. S. West[360]

Years later, items in John's 1823 estate packet relate back to John's 1819 need for funds and refer to John's education in Philadelphia.

> Natchez July 11 1823
> I Gabriel Tichenor Cashier of the Bank of
> the State of Mississippi, do certify that
> according to the Books of entries kept
> at said Bank, a check issued by me as
> Cashier as aforesaid, dated January 8, 1819,
> No. 82, for two hundred dollars on the
> Farmers & Mechanics Bank of Philadelphia
> in favor of John S. West -- that said
> entry is in my hand writing, as is
> correct & true as stated --

---

[356] Ibid., 95-96.

[357] "List of Letters Remaining in the Philadelphia Post-Office, 16 January 1819," *Franklin Gazette* (Philadelphia, Pa.), 18 January 1819, v.2, no.279, p.3, col.5, "John S. West 2"; "List of Letters Remaining in the Philadelphia Post-Office, 31 July 1819," *Franklin Gazette* (Philadelphia, Pa.), 4 August 1819, v.3, no.448, p.1, col.4, "John Smith West 2."

[358] "List of Letters Remaining in the Philadelphia Post-Office, 28 February 1819," *Franklin Gazette*, 1 March 1819, v.3, no.315, p.3, col.5; 3 March 1819, v.3, no.317, p.4, col.3. Letters for "John West" or "Dr. John West" also appeared in issues dated 8 January, v.2, no.279, p.3, col.5; 16, 17, and 19 April; 2, 3, and 4 August; and 17 and 20 September 1819.

[359] "List of Letters Remaining in the Philadelphia Post-Office, 15 September 1819," *Franklin Gazette*, 20 September 1819, v.4, no.488, p.4, col.6. The *Franklin Gazette* continued publication until 1824 (https://www.loc.gov/item/sn84024578/).

[360] Jefferson Co., Miss., Chancery Court, probate packet B-99, John Smith West; FHL microfilm 1,889,020.

Geo. Tichenor [signature]

> I do certify that to the best of my
> knowledge & recollection, and as I verily
> believe, Charles West paid the money
> for the above check, & that the same was
> remited to John S. West, then at Philadel-
> phia, for the benefit of said John S. West
> the better to enable him to obtain his
> education, at Philadelphia --
>   Natchez, July 11, 1823
>   E. Turner [signature][361]

The medical school records show John S. West attended only the one academic year 1818-1819,[362] and settlement of his estate in Mississippi began in early 1821. However, Pennsylvania records account for the deaths of two men named "John S. West" of Philadelphia, one in 1819 and the other in 1820. In the first record, a single-sentence death notice in the 24 September 1819 *Franklin Gazette* stated:

> At sea, on his way from Philadelphia to New Orleans, Dr. John S. West.[363]

In the second record, a 19-year-old John S. West died in Philadelphia of pulmonary consumption on 8 April 1820 and was buried in the New Market Street Baptist burial ground between 9 and 14 April 1820.[364] In 1871, "some 300 bodies were moved" from the Second Baptist Burial Ground, as this cemetery later become known, to Ivy Hill Cemetery also in Philadelphia.[365] Ivy Hill Cemetery does not find a reference to this John West among its card file of every known interment and reinternment in the cemetery's history.[366]

The 24 September 1819 notice of the undated death on an unidentified ship seems the likelier reference to Cato West's son John because it soon follows the end of John's first and only academic year at the University of Pennsylvania, it is contemporaneous with those last letters waiting in the Philadelphia post office for him (perhaps advising him to return home), no further letters were waiting for him after 20 September 1819, and the "Dr." honorific on some letters is apropos of John's field of study, if a bit premature for a first-year medical student. The

---

[361] Ibid.

[362] Email to author from Jim M. Duffin, Senior Archivist and Office Manager, University Archives and Records Center, University of Pennsylvania, Philadelphia, Pa., 21 May 2019.

[363] "Died," *Franklin Gazette* (Philadelphia, Pa.), 24 September 1819, v.4, no.492, p.3, col.1.

[364] Pennsylvania, "Philadelphia City Death Certificates, 1803-1915," *FamilySearch*, digital film 004009772, images 865 and 866 for "John West," series for New Market Street Baptist Burial Ground; image 866 is the death report signed by Dr. Alex. Knight, and image 865 is the burial report signed by sexton Thomas Davis. The 1820-1821 daybook of Dr. Knight does not include John West's name (Historical Medical Library of the College of Physicians of Philadelphia, MSS 412, "Alexander Knight daybooks" finding aid; email to author from Chrissie Perella, 10 May 2019).

[365] Harry Kyriakodis, "Obit for a NoLibs House of Worship," *Hidden City Philadelphia* online newsletter (hiddencityphiladelphia.org), 12 August 2013.

[366] Telephone conversation, 10 May 2019.

shipboard decedent may have had a sea burial, especially if he died from an infectious disease, as extant 1819 Orleans Parish death records do not list him.[367]

On 23 January 1821, Charles West signed a bond as administrator of his brother John's estate in Jefferson County, Miss.[368] Charles filed an "undivided inventory" of John's estate, or "so much of it that has come to [his] possession," on 24 May 1821, listing John's slaves as "Per[?]y, Thamer, Albert, Sarah, Lucy, Philis, Hector, Bill, George, and Mary."[369] A commission appointed in 1826 to make a division of John's estate among his seven legal representatives recommended a sale of John's land and remaining slaves to provide an equitable distribution.[370] The sale record shows brother Benjamin F. West purchased John's 51 2/3 acres of land and four of his slaves: York, blind Sally, Hagar, and Henny/Hany/Harry. Brother and administrator Charles West purchased Sylvia, and brother-in-law Joseph Winn purchased Wat.[371]

John Smith West left no known descendants.

14. RICHARD CLAIBORNE[4] WEST (Cato[3], William[2,1]), son of Cato West and Martha Wills Green,[372] was probably born before 19 April 1804[373] in newly-formed Jefferson County, M.T.,[374] the tenth known child of Cato West[375] by his first wife Martha "Patsey" Wills Green.[376] When Richard was born, his father was Secretary of the Mississippi Territory,[377] and shortly thereafter Acting Governor of the Mississippi Territory.[378]

---

[367] Neither the index to deaths in Orleans Parish, Louisiana, 1804-1838 (FHL microfilm 911,385) nor the actual entries in its "Death Record, 1819-1826," from July-September 1819 (pages 4-26; FHL microfilm 900,241) include the 1819 shipboard death of John S. West, which the passenger ship should have reported upon arrival there.

[368] Jefferson Co., Miss., Chancery Court, probate packet B-99, John S. West; FHL microfilm 1,889,020.

[369] Ibid, "Inventory of the Estate of Jno. S. West," 24 May 1821.

[370] Ibid, Commission's report, 27 February 1826.

[371] Ibid, "Act. Sales of John S. West Estate," 25 April 1826.

[372] Jefferson Co., Miss., Will Book A:24-25, will of Cato West names "Richard Claiborne" West as one of his six youngest children.

[373] Jefferson Co., Miss., Deed Book A:205 (p.389 of the typed transcription), Richard C. West to Charles West, 19 April 1825; FHL microfilm 892,554. Clara Joorfetz, State Librarian of the Mississippi State Law Library, confirmed that the section "under 'Orphan's Court' Ch. 9 p.32" of the 1824 revised state code "says a male, age 21 or female age 18 may inherit property – which would imply they could sell it also"; email to author dated 16 October 2013. Since Richard C. West was selling inherited property in April 1825, his birth likely occurred by April 1804.

[374] Jefferson Co., Miss., Deed Book B1:44 (p.33 of the typed transcription), Cato and Patsey West et al. to Everard Green, 1 April 1804, recorded 25 February 1805; FHL microfilm 892,552.

[375] Jefferson Co., Miss., Will Book A:24-25, will of Cato West, 30 July 1818.

[376] Green family Bible transcription in supporting documentation for NSDAR nat. no. 373,979, 13. The transcription includes multiple generations descending from the 12 children of Col. Green (b.1723) and Martha Wills (b.1734), without listing birth, marriage, or death dates or places for most individuals (births from 1723 and deaths to 1859). The accompanying 8 December 1947 affidavit (digital image 6372029) states that the transcriptions were "true copies" made by the Bible's former owner Evelyn (Cox) Inge of Meridian, Miss.; the original Bible was in 1947 in the possession of her daughter-in-law, Mrs. John Inge Jr. of Ridgewood, N.J. Two written inquiries to a grandson of John Inge Jr. about the current location of the original Green family Bible went unanswered.

[377] Dunbar Rowland, ed., *The Official and Statistical Register of the State of Mississippi, 1904* (Nashville, Tenn.: Brandon Printing Co., 1904), 109.

[378] Rowland, *The Official and Statistical Register of the State of Mississippi,* 1904, 109.

Richard was about age fifteen when his father Cato West died testate in 1819. Twenty-eight-year-old Charles West served as guardian of the interests of his minor full brothers Richard C. and Benjamin F. West.[379] By 19 April 1825, Richard had apparently reached age twenty-one as he sold to his brother Charles the four slaves their late father left to him, his interest in his late brother John S. West's property, and any real property devised to him in their father's will.[380] On 25 November 1826, he signed a receipt for his $1,360 share of his late father's estate:

> Rec'd of Charles West my guardian thirteen
> hundred and sixty dollars __ cents in full of
> my estate;
> Nov. 25 1826
> R. C. West.[381]

Richard was not located in the federal census of 1830, or any other census year through 1860.[382] The next known record places him about 100 miles northeast of Jefferson County. "R. C. West" appeared on an 1832 tax list of Yazoo County, Mississippi, sharing an entry with his similarly aged nephew J[ames]. R[aiford]. West.[383] Their entry appears three lines above Richard's older widowed sister Ann (West) Winn's, all assessed for personal property only, suggesting none owned real property.[384]

Either the author or the transcriber of the original Green family Bible entries mistakenly listed "Claborne" with his brother Charles's wife (Charlotte Neely) rather than his own.[385] No marriage record for Richard C. West appears in Jefferson County records.[386] Published Clay and Ewing family genealogies assert, incorrectly, that Cato's son "Claiborne" West died unmarried.[387]

---

[379] Jefferson Co., Miss., Chancery Court, probate packet B-90, R. C. West, guardian bond of Charles West, 23 January 1821; FHL microfilm 1,889,020. George Poindexter, *The revised code of the laws of Mississippi, in which are comprised all such acts of the General Assembly, of a public nature, as were in force at the end of the year, 1823; with a general index* (Natchez, printed by Francis Baker, 1824), 68; Chapter 9, Orphans' Court, Section 135: "The powers and duties of every testamentary or other guardian, over the person and estate of the ward, shall cease and determine, when such ward shall either arrive at the age of twenty-one years, or be lawfully married . . . ."

[380] Jefferson Co., Miss., Deed Book A:205 (p.389 of typed version), Richard C. West to Charles West, 19 April 1825; FHL microfilm 892,554. The slaves included Annonet (about age twenty-five), Rhoda (about seven), Isaac (about fifteen), and Joe (about one).

[381] Jefferson Co., Miss., Chancery Court, probate packet B-90, R. C. West; FHL microfilm 1,889,020. Receipt of R. C. West, 25 November 1826, includes his original signature.

[382] *Ancestry* (http://search.ancestry.com). Searches included a ten-year range in birth date with and without a Mississippi birthplace.

[383] Son of the late William West (d.1810). Jefferson Co., Miss., Chancery Court, probate packet A-79, "W[illiam]. West."

[384] *FamilySearch* (www.familysearch.org), "Mississippi, State Archives, Various Records, 1820-1951; Yazoo, County tax rolls, 1823-1832, Box 3800," digital film 4854376, image 353, no page number, 1832 combined assessment, "J.R. & R.C. West" (seventh entry on page) and "Ann Winn" (tenth entry on page).

[385] Green family Bible transcription in supporting documentation for NSDAR nat. no. 373,979, p.13. Also see Jefferson Co., Miss., Marriage Licenses and Certificates, A:154, West-Neely, 6 June 1820; FHL microfilm 893,070.

[386] Jefferson Co., Miss., Marriage Licenses and Certificates, vol. A, negative search; FHL microfilm 893,070.

[387] Zachary F. Smith and Mary Rogers Clay, *The Clay Family* (Louisville, Ky.: The Filson Club, 1899), 224. Also see Presley Kittredge Ewing and Mary Ellen (Williams) Ewing, *The Ewing Genealogy with Cognate Branches – A Survey of the Ewings and Their Kin in America* (Houston, Tex.: by the compilers, 1919), 140.

By 16 October 1833 Richard, nearly thirty years old, had married AMELIA TRAHERN, who had claimed land as a Choctaw "orphan child."[388] Then yet a teenager, Amelia was born about 1817[389] to Wesley Trahern[390] and his Choctaw-descendant wife Delilah Brashears.[391] No West–Trahern marriage record survives in Yazoo or Holmes County,[392] the latter formed from Yazoo County in 1833.[393] Richard C. West continued to be taxed in Holmes County from 1833 through 1837, listed as a resident of "Harland's Creek" in 1837.[394]

Richard appeared as a defendant in an 1838 Holmes County lawsuit before his family's departure that year to Texas. In January 1838, Erasmus Potts sued Elias F. Deloach (the second husband of Richard's sister Ann), Joseph W. Deloach (Elias's brother), Richard C. West, Vestal Caraway, and James Enloe.[395] To satisfy the judgment Potts won, the sheriff sold land belonging to the Deloach brothers.[396] The case records do not survive and the sheriff's deed does not record where Richard lived at that time. The family resided in Holmes County as late as 2 April 1838,

---

[388] *Letters Received by the Office of Indian Affairs, 1824-81* (Washington, D.C.: National Archives and Records Service, 1959), NARA microfilm M234, roll 188, frame 624, F. E. Plummer, 27 March 1835: "States that Amelia L., wife of Richd. C. West, formerly Amelia L. Trahern, has had assigned her . . .[land] as orphan under the provisions of the 19 Art. Dancing Rabbit Ck...."; roll 190 (1838-1840), frame 382, Hon. F. E. Plummer, 3 April 1838: "Address him [Plummer] at 'Tchula, Holmes Co., Mi.'"; frames 387-388, "Choctaw Agency Reserve, 1833-1860," letter of Amelia L. West to William Trahern Esq., 16 October 1833). The clue to this marriage appeared in "Descendants of Wesley Trahern, Choctaw Nation, MS" (http://jenniferhsrn2.homestead.com/Wesley.html).

[389] 1860 U.S. census, Fayette County, Texas, LaGrange, p 301-B stamped and p.86 written, dwelling 649, family 819, "Emelia Thall" [*sic*] (age forty-three); NARA M653, roll 1294. Amelia had remarried to Rev. Thrall by this date.

[390] *FamilySearch* (www.familysearch.org), "Mississippi, Probate Records 1781-1930," digital images, Probate Records 1825-1922, Mississippi, Chancery Court (Hinds County), Old Series Estates (series 1) 1825, no.0-37, digital film 5815544, images 608-611, Estate no. 17 of Wesley Trahern; petition of James H. Kerr, administrator de bonis non, 1 November 1844, identifying the children of the deceased, including "Amelia who has since intermarried with Claiborne C. West who are supposed to reside in the Republic of Texas."

[391] U.S. Congress, *American State Papers: Documents, Legislative and Executive of the Congress of the United States*, part 8, vol. 7 (Washington, D.C.: Gale and Seaton, 1860), 38; W. Ward to Elbert Herring Esq., 19 October 1832. For citations to evidence of Delilah's parents as Zadoc Brashear(s) and Susannah Vaughan, including her 1794 Baton Rouge baptism citation, see Charles Brashear's "Delilah Brashears and Wesley Trahern," *A Brashear(s) Family History, Descendants of Robert and Benois Basseur, Vol. 5, Two Brashear(s) Families of the Lower Mississippi Valley, Their Choctaw, & Other Descendants*, (Santa Rosa, Calif.: by the author, 2002), 387.

[392] Extant marriage records begin in 1845 in Yazoo County and in 1884 in Holmes County; MDAH Collections (http://opac2.mdah.state.ms.us/county/mfcounty1.php).

[393] "An Act to Divide the County of Yazoo," passed 19 February 1833, *Laws of the State of Mississippi Embracing All Acts of a Public Nature from January Session, 1824, to January 1838, Inclusive* (Jackson, Miss.: by authority, 1838), 466-468.

[394] Holmes Co., Miss., Tax Lists, Richard C. West; digital images, "Mississippi, State Archives, Various Records 1820-1951," database, Holmes, County tax rolls 1833-1846, Box 3658, *FamilySearch* (www.familysearch.org); 1833, combined assessment, p.20 (image 23), Richard C. West, one poll; 1834, combined assessment, p.17 (image 47), Richard C. West, one poll (between entries for Ann Winn and James R. West); 1835, combined assessment, no pagination (image 75), Richard C. West, one poll (between entries for James R. West and Ann Winn); 1836, combined assessment, p.26 (image 106), Richard C. West, one white poll (follows entry for James R. West); 1837, combined assessment, p.19 (image 130), Richard C. West, situation "Harlan[d]'s C[reek]," one white poll, five slaves (precedes entry for James R. West, situation Yazoo Valley). No entry for Richard C. West in the next available tax list, dated 1840.

[395] Holmes Co., Miss., Deed Book G:295, Sheriff John D. Wyatt to John Bennett, 19 October 1842; FHL microfilm 879,462. The text of the deed refers to January 1838 court case.

[396] Ibid.

when a resident wrote to the Office of Indian Affairs regarding the Choctaw land of sisters Letha (Trahern) Lane and Amelia (Trahern) West, identifying both as Holmes County citizens.[397]

Later that year, Richard and Amelia removed to the Republic of Texas,[398] an independent nation between the time of the Alamo and the Mexican War.[399] Richard West and Amelia's brother-in-law Cornelius Lane rented the league of land (4,428 acres) originally granted to Plácido Benavides in Victoria County.[400] By 1840 they had set up a merchandise forwarding company in Linnville, on Lavaca Bay.[401] The 7 July 1840 tax list of Victoria County revealed few Linville landowners; only six household heads owned town lots solely in Linnville, and three others had assessments including additional town lots in Victoria (and thus may not have been residing in Linnville).[402] Cornelius Lane, not a landowner, was assessed for two white males over age twenty-one, presumably himself and Richard C. West, and "Cornelius Lane & Co." was assessed for one saddle horse, two pleasure carriages, and three slaves.[403]

A month later, on 8 August 1840, Comanche Indians attacked Linnville, killing or kidnapping several of its inhabitants, slaughtering livestock, and destroying the town.[404] Some fleeing residents sought immediate refuge in boats on the bay. A Linnville resident's eyewitness account noted, "The amiable families of Messrs. Lane and West fortunately reached the boats without misfortune."[405] Amelia may have provided firsthand memories of that fateful day to her second husband, who wrote an account of the attack decades later in his history of Texas.[406]

After the attack, Richard West served as Deputy Collector of Linnville's re-emerging port.[407] In the Vasquez campaign in early 1842, he was also an assistant commissary and quartermaster sergeant of the Victoria County Volunteers under Captain John Price and Colonel Owen.[408]

---

[397] *Letters Received by the Office of Indian Affairs, 1824-81;* NARA M234, roll 190, frame 383, F. E. Plummer to Cary A. Harris, Esq., Commissioner Indian Affairs, 2 April 1838. "Amelia L. West, wife of Richard C. West, formerly Amelia L. Trahern alias Amelia Trahern & Letha H. Lane wife of Cornelius Lane formerly Letha H. Trahern alias Letha Trahern *citizens of the county of Holmes & state of Mississippi,* are two of the persons claiming land . . ." [emphasis added].

[398] Texas, "Land Grants," database and digital images, *Texas General Land Office* (http://www.glo.texas.gov/cf/ land-grant-search), Richard West, 1846, File 980, Bexar County, two surveys (640 acres total), image 7 of 7. G. W. Palmer certification signed on 6 July 1846, Victoria County, stating that West "arrived in this State during the time of Republic in the Year 1838, that he is a married man . . . ."

[399] Joseph Milton Nance, "Republic of Texas," *Handbook of Texas*, Texas State Historical Association (https://www.tshaonline.org/handbook/online/articles/mzr02).

[400] *DeLeón, A Tejano Family History* (Austin: University of Texas Press, 2003), 202, fn 34, citing the "Estate of Placido Benavides, 8 June 1838, vol. 2, p.43-46, Probate Records; Victoria County Clerk's Office."

[401] "Notice," *Times-Picayune* (New Orleans), 4 September 1840, p.3, col.5.

[402] Gifford White, *The 1840 Census of the Republic of Texas* (Austin: Pemberton Press, 1966), 200-204.

[403] Ibid., 202.

[404] "Burning of Linnville by the Indians," *Public Ledger* (Philadelphia, Pa.), 23 September 1840, v.9, no.153, p.1, col.6; as reprinted from the *New Orleans Bulletin.*

[405] Ibid.

[406] Rev. Homer S. Thrall, "Comanche Invasion," *A Pictorial History of Texas from the Earliest Visits of European Adventurers to A.D. 1883* (St. Louis: N. D. Thompson & Co., 1883), 465.

[407] "From Texas," *The Daily Picayune* (New Orleans, La.), 25 March 1842, v.1, no.52, p.2, col.3.

[408] Texas, Republic Claims, database and digital images, "Republic Claims Database," no.1343, A. S. McDonald, Texas State Library and Archives Commission (http://www.tsl.state.tx.us), citing reel 171, p.545 (Set 1, image 17100545).

Mr. West, the Deputy Collector, had just come in from camp and reports, "A spy company had just come in who had seen a large body of Mexicans, supposed to be 9,000, fifteen miles west of the Nueces, and then on the march. There were two wagons at Linnville pressing every article in the way of provisions for our army."[409]

Newspaper accounts in 1844 show Richard was the Deputy Collector also at Port "La Baca" (Lavaca), a few miles southeast of Linnville.[410] When Calhoun County was formed from Victoria County in 1846, he served briefly as the new county's first sheriff.[411]

Richard paid taxes in Calhoun County for the first and last time in 1846.[412] His tax assessment identifies his property and that of William Lane and Charles West, for whom Richard acted as agent.[413] On 6 July 1846, Richard appeared before the Board of Land Commissioners back in Victoria County.[414] As a married man who had arrived in the Republic in 1838, West qualified for a land grant, and obtained an "unconditional certificate" redeemable for 640 acres.[415] The same day, he assigned the grant to Samuel Maverick for $30.[416]

Richard fell ill in early spring 1847. Dr. Moses Johnson applied blood-letting procedures on 29 and 30 March, followed by "24 hour attention" from 3 through 11 April 1847, presumably when the 43-year-old patient died.[417] A brief death notice appeared in the New Orleans *Daily Picayune* on 4 May 1847: "'From Texas' . . . The deaths of Mr. George Parr and Mr. Richard West, at Port Lavaca, are announced."[418] Richard's remains were interred in the Ranger Cemetery in Port Lavaca, according to a daughter's obituary, although no tombstone survives.[419] He did not leave a will.

The 1847 Calhoun County tax list assessed "Mrs. West admr. for R. West" for one town lot on Indian Point in Port Lavaca, worth $1,200, and 150 head of cattle, worth $600.[420] On 5 June

[409] *Daily Picayune* (New Orleans, La.), 25 March 1842, v.1, no.52, p.2, col.3.

[410] "Joint Resolution for the relief of Richard West, Deputy Collector at the Port of La Baca," *Telegraph and Texas Register* (Houston, Tex.), 6 March 1844, v.9, no.12, p.1, col.1; The Portal to Texas History (https://texashistory .unt.edu/ark:/67531/metapth78040/m1/1/?q=richard%20west).

[411] Historical Records Survey. Texas, *Inventory of the County Archives of Texas: Calhoun County, no. 29* (January 1941), 7; digital images, *The Portal to Texas History* (http://texashistory.unt.edu), citing University of North Texas Libraries, Denton, Texas. Footnote 43 cites "County Court Journal, vol. A, p.1, in Minutes Commissioners Court" for West's service as sheriff.

[412] *FamilySearch* (www.familysearch.org), "Texas, County Tax Rolls 1846-1910," database, Calhoun County, 1846, image 6, no page number, Richd. West.

[413] Ibid.

[414] Texas, "Land Grants," *Texas General Land Office*, File 980, Bexar County, Richard West, 1846.

[415] Ibid., certificate no. 47.

[416] Ibid. This document image includes his original signature.

[417] Calhoun Co., Texas, Probate File 1847-4, account of Dr. Moses Johnson, n.d.; County Clerk, Port Lavaca, Texas. The Papers of Moses Johnson (accession no.1926, Dolph Briscoe Center for American History, University of Texas, Austin, Tex.) did not include patient records or charges (email to author, 18 June 2012, from Sarah Traugott, Reference Intern).

[418] "From Texas," *Daily Picayune* (New Orleans, La.), 4 May 1847, v.11, no.85, p.2, col.2. The same notice also appeared in Philadelphia's *North American* and Albany, New York's, *Evening Journal* on 13 May 1847, and in the *New-York (City) Spectator* on 15 May 1847.

[419] "Death of Mrs. Thornton," *Galveston Daily News* (Galveston, Tex.), 31 October 1868, v.5, no.55, p.1, col.1.

[420] *FamilySearch* (www.familysearch.org), "Texas, County Tax Rolls 1846-1910," database, Calhoun County, 1847, images 9 and 18, no page numbers, "Mrs. West admx. of R. West."

1847, the court appointed Amelia administratrix of her late husband's estate.[421] She stated in one of her petitions, ". . . said Decedent left two children who are minors [Martha Lavinia and Laura O.] and are the children of your petitioner and compose part of her family."[422]

Amelia and her two children do not appear in the 1850 federal census, although she paid tax in Calhoun County that year.[423] She remarried there in 1852 to Methodist minister and future author Homer S. Thrall.[424] A severe cholera outbreak struck Calhoun County in 1852 and 1853 when Amelia and her new husband came to the aid of those afflicted:

> Last year [1853], Thrall was in Indianola [in Calhoun County] during the whole epidemic ministering to the temporal and spiritual wants of the sick. His wife—Heaven bless her—left her little ones to attend the dying. We cannot forget their kind attention to our own family when all of us were sick and two lay dying. . . .At one time Mrs. Thrall kept vigil for 30 hours without closing her eyes.[425]

The presence of such pestilence or the absence of educational opportunities in Texas may have prompted the Thralls to send Amelia's older child—Martha Lavinia West—to boarding school in Mississippi in the late 1850s. But there she died, along with her roommate, Mary Whitney:

> Died at Rodney, [Jefferson County, Mississippi,] on the 1st of April [1857], Miss Martha Lavinia West, in the sixteenth year of her age, she was the daughter of the late Richard Claiborne West, youngest [sic] son of Col. Cato West of this county.
> This lovely and interesting girl was a victim to that fell destroy-r consumption. This disease was constracted by her whilst a student at Franklin Female College, Holly Springs [in north Mississippi.] [W]e all remember with what joyous and bouyant hopes[] Lavinia with three other companions left our neighborhood last Autumn to finish her well founded education at the above named institution. Alas! alas! two of that small number are now in the silent tomb, they are beyond the reach of neglect, or the need of a mother's care. . . .   R.[426] [Spelling as in original.]

---

[421] Texas State Library and Archives Commission (https://www.tsl.texas.gov/apps/arc/repclaims/ index.php), digital images, "Republic Claims," no.1343, includes claims for A. S. McDonald and the late Richard West. West's widow Amelia L. West gave power of attorney to D. M. Stapp "to demand, receive, and receipt for, any and all sums of money due and owing to me as the Heir of my said husband's Estate from the State of Texas"; citing reel 171, p.552, Set 2 image 17100552. She received $42.70 for Richard West's "services as Q[uarte]r. M[aste]r Serg[ean]t on the Vasquez Campaign under Col. C[lark]. L. Owen in 1842," for one month and 12 days (reel 171, Set 1, image 17100546).

[422] Calhoun Co., Texas, Probate File 1847-4, Richard C. West, petition of widow and administratrix Amelia West, 29 September 1848; photocopies, Port Lavaca, Tex.

[423] *FamilySearch* (www.familysearch.org), "Texas, County Tax Rolls 1846-1910," database, Calhoun County, 1850, image 8, no page number, Amelia West. She was assessed on town lots no. 5, 6, and 7 in block no. 7 in Lavaca worth $1,000; 1 Negro $300; 20 cattle $100, for a total value of $1,400.

[424] *FamilySearch* (www.familysearch.org), "Texas, County Marriages Index, 1837-1977," index, Calhoun County, "Marriage Records, 1846-1919," H. S. Thrall and Amelia West, 21 July 1852; citing FHL microfilm 1,011,210.

[425] Paul Freier, "Epidemics Horrors [sic] in County," *Port Lavaca Wave*, 13 April 1977; an image of this article clipping appears on page 62 of Paul H. Freier's *A "Looking Back" Scrapbook for Calhoun County and Matagorda Bay, Texas* (Port Lavaca, Texas: Port Lavaca Wave, 1979). Neither the identity of the informant quoted in the above passage nor a citation to the newspaper publishing the firsthand account appears in the clipped article, which includes a portrait of Amelia (Trahern) West Thrall.

[426] Martha Lavinia West obituary, *Fayette Watch Tower* (Fayette, Miss.), 17 April 1857, page number undetermined; MDAH microfilm 20436; Mississippi State Archives, Jackson. A transcription of this obituary available online

The roommate's bereaved father wrote to the editor of Jefferson County, Mississippi's, *Fayette Watch Tower*, critical of the attending physician's care of both girls:

> I observed in your issue of the 10th inst. an article over the signature of D. J. Allen referring to an obituary notice of my daughter, Mary Whitney . . . Miss West, another pupil of Dr. Allen and roommate of Mary, whose health was delicate, being a victim to consumption of which she died about 2-weeks since, said on her death bed at home, that while at Holly Springs she asked Dr. Allen to take her as far as Rodney while on his way to a conference at Waterproof, La. She says she was told that Waterproof was above Rodney and he could not take her, when she knew Rodney was some distance above. Her dying words, "Mother, we must all try to pray to forgive Dr. Allen for his neglect of Mary Whitney and myself."[427]

On 2 April 1857, family consigned Lavinia's remains to the Fayette Cemetery section in which her uncle Charles had recently buried three deceased children. Lavinia's tombstone identifies her as a daughter of "R.C. & A. West."[428] John Darden attended the burial, according to Susan (Sillers) Darden's diary:

> April 3 [1857]: ...Cousin John Darden was here[.] [He] was at Lavenia West['s] burying yesterday[.] [S]he died with consumption[.] [S]he came home from Holly Springs with it[.] [H]er mother lives in Texas[.] [S]he came for her[.] [S]he started back home, got to Rodney with her[, and] she died suddenly.[429]

---

omits the word "late" from the phrase "the late Richard Claiborne West"; *USGenWeb Archives* (http://files.usgwarchives.net/ms/jefferson/newspaper/watc1857.txt). Lynna Kay Shudfield, abstractor, "Gleanings from Fayette Watch-Tower & Jefferson Journal, Jefferson County, Mississippi," database (http://jeffersoncountyms .org/Newspapers/Watchtower.htm), citing MDAH microfilm roll M106, Mississippi State Archives Newspaper Collection, Jackson. The transcription of J. M. Whitney's letter to the editor is cited as appearing in the 29 April 1857 issue. Note that Richard was not the youngest son of Cato West. The fact that Martha Lavinia died *and* was buried in Jefferson County, Mississippi, may indicate that her family sent her (and possibly her younger sister Laura O.) from Texas back to her uncle Charles West's home for schooling. Charles West was Richard C. West's only surviving full sibling by 1850. The 1857 personal tax roll of Jefferson County, which does not distinguish residents of Rodney, included Charles West but does not record Homer Thrall, any Traherns, or the late Richard C. West's remarried sister-in-law Gabriella (Johnston) West Tilden; *FamilySearch* (www.familysearch.org) "Mississippi, State Archives, Various Records, 1820-1951," database, County tax rolls, 1857, Box 3672, Jefferson, image 59, p.25, Charles West.

[427] Shudfield, "Gleanings from Fayette Watch-Tower," 29 April 1857.

[428] Brown, *Jefferson Co., Miss., Cemeteries, Etc.*, 2:99: Fayette Cemetery, Section M. She was buried among three predeceasing children of her uncle Charles West.

[429] Susan (Sillers) Darden, Diary (Jefferson Co., Miss., 9 June 1853–31 December 1861), vol. 1, unpaginated, 3 April 1857 entry; Darden Family Papers (Z/0082.000), MDAH microfilm roll 35992; Mississippi State Archives, Jackson. The entry for this date, copied from the microfilmed original diary, is considerably longer than the Kevin Ross Richland transcription PDFs found online (http://jeffersoncountyms.org/dardendiary.htm). Mrs. Darden's diary entry of 27 August 1856 identified "Lavinia West" as one of four students (including Mary Whitney) sailing from Rodney to Holly Springs for school, which matches information in her 1857 obituary and further supports the theory that Martha Lavinia West may have been boarding with her uncle Charles West. The Rare Book librarian at Emory University's Manuscript, Archives, and Rare Book Library confirmed that the student listings in their *Catalogue of the Officers and Students of Franklin Female College, Holly Springs, Miss., 1854-1855* (Holly Springs, Miss.: Mississippi Times Cheap Book and Job Print, 1855) do not include Martha Lavinia West, whose entry might have named her Texas home town; email from David Faulds to author, 19 November 2013.

Shortly after Lavinia's death, in 1859, her uncle Charles bequeathed $1,500 to "my niece, Laura West, daughter of my brother Richard Claiborne West."[430] By 1860, the Thralls resided in Fayette County, Texas, with 16-year-old Laura O. West.[431] After the Civil War, the Thralls returned to Calhoun County, Texas, where Laura married an aspiring Galveston newspaper man, John E. Thornton, on 10 December 1867, with stepfather Rev. Thrall officiating.[432] Thornton's comrades on another Galveston newspaper published a wedding notice with collegial insight and humor:

> A Happy Brother—Mr. John E. Thornton, the local of our cotemporary, the daily News, has returned from Lavaca, this morning, on the steamship I. C. Harris, and a neat white package of bridal cake tied in snow white satin ribbon, found lying on our table this morning aroused a realization of the result. Accompanying was the card, we saw it all at A glance. At that place on Dec. 10th, he was United in wedlock to Miss Laura O. West, and brings his wife to live among us. We congratulate the newly married couple. May life be to them a clean copy, and all items of a quiet and wholesome nature, and when a proof is taken of their matrimonial bliss in this commercial world, may it require no alteration or erasure.[433]

Thornton's co-workers applied their insider knowledge in a more mournful piece just ten months later:

> From our Evening Edition of Yesterday
> DEATH OF MRS. THORNTON—Our commercial editor, Mr. John E. Thornton, has just returned to the city from the sad task of consigning to the tomb the remains of his beautiful and accomplished wife, formerly Miss Laura O. West, daughter of Major West, an old Texan, and stepdaughter of Rev. H. E. [sic] Thrall. She died at Victoria, whither she had gone in search of health, on Sunday night [25 October 1868], and her remains were conveyed in a metallic coffin to Lavaca, where she was buried on Wednesday morning, by the side of her father.
> No more lovely or affectionate woman was ever torn by death from the heart and home of a devoted husband. . . .[434]

The ill-fated Laura may have met Thornton through the editorial enterprises of her stepfather, Rev. Homer S. Thrall, editor of the *Lavaca Commercial* newspaper at the time.[435] Rev. Thrall "served terms as presiding elder and circuit preacher in several districts in both the Texas

---

[430] Jefferson Co., Miss., Will Book B:61-63, Charles West will, 19 April 1859, codicil dated 22 August 1859; FHL microfilm 893,068. The testator had other orphaned minor nephews and nieces, including another similarly-aged Laura O. West (daughter of Benjamin F. West, deceased), for whom he did not provide. A receipt signed by Laura O. West (daughter of Richard C. West) or her guardian in Texas may exist in Charles West's Chancery Court probate packet D-182; however, that packet is missing from the courthouse and from the FHL microfilmed sequence of Chancery Court packets (FHL microfilm 1,905,384).

[431] 1860 U.S. census, Fayette Co., Texas, p.301-B stamped and p.86 written, dwelling 649, family 819, Laura O. West; NARA microfilm M653, roll 1294.

[432] Calhoun County, Texas, Marriage Records, Book A:278, license no. 419, John E. Thornton and Laura O. West, 10 December 1867; FHL microfilm 1,011,210.

[433] "Local Intelligence," *Flake's Semi-Weekly Galveston Bulletin* (Galveston, Tex.), 18 December 1867, v.5, no.71, p.5, col.1.

[434] *Galveston Daily News*, 31 October 1868, p.1, col.1.

[435] "About the Lavaca Commercial," *Chronicling America* (http://chroniclingamerica.loc.gov/lccn/sn86090139/).

Conference and the West Texas Conference" until 1891 and found time to write "five widely read" books: *History of Methodism in Texas* (1872), *A History of Texas* (1876), *A Pictorial History of Texas* (1879), *The People's Illustrated Almanac, Texas Handbook, and Immigrants' Guide* (1880), and *A Brief History of Methodism in Texas* (1889).[436] "Among the districts in which he preached were Rutersville, Galveston, Austin, Victoria, Houston, Corpus Christi, San Antonio, Seguin, and Del Rio."[437] Rev. Thrall died 12 October 1894 in San Antonio,[438] having "willed his library of 2,300 volumes to Southwestern University."[439]

The 1900 federal census noted tht the widowed Amelia (Trahern) West Thrall had outlived five children.[440] This suggests that she and Richard had three children who died young, probably during the first nine years of their marriage, as available evidence indicates that Amelia had no children with her second husband. Accounts of the 8 August 1840 Comanche raid on Linnville mention no West children among the casualties.

Amelia (Trahern) West Thrall died on 22 July 1905 in San Antonio, Texas.[441] A long death notice incorrectly gave her name as "Amanda," the name of Homer Thrall's first wife.[442] It described her life with Rev. Thrall without giving her birth name or date, identifying her first husband, or referring to her then-deceased children.[443]

The correlated data demonstrate that the 1847 Texas decedent was Cato West's son and that he married and had children. That Richard C. West's offspring apparently produced no surviving grandchild may account for this family branch fading from the memories and records of his close kin.

The children of Richard Claiborne[4] West and Amelia Trahern:

Perhaps i.   (UNKNOWN)[5] WEST, born about 1835; died before April 1847.
Perhaps ii.   (UNKNOWN) WEST, born about 1837; died before April 1847.
Perhaps iii. (UNKNOWN) WEST, born about 1839; died before April 1847.

---

[436] Norman W. Spellmann, "Thrall, Homer Spellman," *Handbook of Texas Online* (http://www.tshaonline.org /handbook/online/articles/fth35). Published by the Texas State Historical Association.
[437] Spellmann, "Thrall, Homer Spellman." See also 1870 U.S. census, Harris Co., Texas, 3rd Ward Houston, p.550 stamped and p.6 written, dwelling 46, family 50; NARA M593, roll 1589; and 1880 U.S. census, Nueces Co., Texas, City of Corpus Christi, ED 116, p.10D stamped and p.20 written, dwelling and family 185, Mesquit St.; NARA T9, roll 1611.
[438] "Mortuary, Rev. H. S. Thrall," *The Galveston Daily News* (Galveston, Tex.), 13 October 1894, v.53, no.204, p.1, col.7.
[439] Spellmann, "Thrall, Homer Spellman."
[440] 1900 U.S. census, Bexar Co., Texas, San Antonio City, Precinct no. 9, ED 91, p.14B, 220 Belvin St., dwelling 252, family 279, Amelia Thrall; NARA T523, roll 1611.
[441] "Aged Citizen Dead— Mrs. Amanda Thrall, Widow of Late Author, Dies at Hospital Saturday Night," *San Antonio Express* (San Antonio, Tex.), 23 July 1905, v.40, no.204, p.11, col.5. *Find A Grave* (findagrave.com), Amelia Trahern Thrall, 1905, memorial 30535419 by "Carol" in 2008 (City Cemetery #2, San Antonio, Bexar County, Texas). Biographical information without source citations (posted by "Jennifer") accompanies the anonymously posted photograph.
[442] Washington Co., Texas, Marriages, 1:11, Homer S. Thrall and Amanda Kerr, 29 June 1847; FHL microfilm 956,482.
[443] "Aged Citizen Dead— Mrs. Amanda Thrall, Widow of Late Author, Dies at Hospital Saturday Night," *San Antonio Express*, 23 July 1905.

iv.   MARTHA LAVINIA WEST, born about 1841-1842[444] in Victoria Co., Republic of Texas; died Rodney, Jefferson Co., Miss., 1 April 1857;[445] buried in Fayette Cemetery, Fayette, Miss.[446]

v.   LAURA O. WEST, born 1843[447] in Victoria Co., Republic of Texas; married John E. Thornton on 10 December 1867 in Calhoun Co., Tex.;[448] died 25 October 1868 in Victoria Co., Tex.;[449] buried in Ranger Cemetery, Port Lavaca, Calhoun Co., Tex.[450] The long *Galveston Daily News* obituary published for Laura O. (West) Thornton did not mention any child born during the ten months she was married, thus it does not appear that she had surviving issue.

15. BENJAMIN FRANKLIN[4] WEST (Cato[3], William[2,1]), son of Cato West and Martha Wills Green,[451] was born 13 March 1805[452] in Jefferson County, M.T.[453] When Benjamin was only thirteen years old, his older brother Thomas West died, leaving all of his real and personal estate to Benjamin, with certain exceptions.[454] These bequests presumably would include as much of the 427 acres Thomas had from his father in 1815 that remained in his hands at his death.[455] Nevertheless, it was their father Cato West who later in 1818 conveyed to Benjamin, for love and affection, two and one-half acres of land on which stood Thomas's "dwelling house and other improvements."[456]

The guardianship accounts filed for Benjamin F. West's share of his late father's estate provide the little that is known of Benjamin's youth: doctors' bills in 1822, F. Stanton & Co.'s store accounts paid in 1823, and $200 "cash remitted to Kentucky" in 1825, which may hint at his college education there.[457] Benjamin F. West signed a receipt on 25 November 1826 for $1,206

---

[444] Her obituary states she was "in her 16th year" at her death on 1 April 1857, which means she had reached her 15th birthday but not her 16th, placing her birth between 2 April 1841 and 31 March 1842.

[445] Martha Lavinia West obituary, *Fayette Watch Tower*, 17 April 1857.

[446] Brown, *Jefferson Co., Miss., Cemeteries, Etc.*, 2:99.

[447] *Find A Grave* (www.findagrave.com), Laura West Thornton, 1843-1868, memorial 10847538 by Jerry Spicer; photograph by Lanny Medlin (Ranger Cemetery, Port Lavaca, Calhoun County, Texas). "Born 1843, Married 1867, Died 1868."

[448] Calhoun Co., Texas, Marriages, A:278, Thornton–West, 10 December 1867; FHL microfilm 1,011,210. "Local Intelligence," *Flake's Semi-Weekly Galveston Bulletin*, Wednesday, 18 December 1867, p.5, col.1.

[449] *Galveston Daily News*, 31 October 1868, p.1, col.1.

[450] *Find A Grave,* photograph, gravestone for Laura West Thornton (1843-1868), Port Lavaca, Tex.

[451] Jefferson Co., Miss., Will Book A:24-25, will of Cato West names "Benjamin Franklin" West as one of his six youngest children.

[452] *Find a Grave* (www.findagrave.com), Benjamin Franklin West, 22 August 1845, memorial 5636955, by William Sanders; photograph (Wintergreen Cemetery, Claiborne Co., Miss.). "Born March 13, 1805." Also, 1845 obituary says in 41st year, indicating 1805.

[453] 1805 territorial census of Cato West. Benjamin F. West should have been age twenty-one when he signed a receipt for his share of his father's estate from his guardian (brother Charles West) on 25 November 1826 (Chancery Court packet B-91, Benjamin F. West; FHL microfilm 1,889,020). The last known living date for his mother, Martha Wills (Green) West, is 1 April 1804 when she joined in a deed with some of her siblings (Jefferson Co., Miss., Deed Book B1:44 (p.33 of the typed transcription), Cato and Patsey West et al. to Everard Green, 1 April 1804, recorded 25 February 1805; FHL microfilm 892,552).

[454] Jefferson Co., Miss., Will Book A:23, will of Thomas West, 18 August 1812.

[455] Jefferson Co., Miss., Deed Book C1:168.

[456] Jefferson Co., Miss., Deed Book A:25 (typed deed book page 46).

[457] Jefferson Co., Miss., Chancery Court, probate packet B-91, Benjamin F. West; FHL microfilm 1,889,020.

he received from his guardian (brother Charles West) for the sale of a mare, a yoke of oxen, and two slaves—Anthony and Charles.[458]

On 16 April 1829, James A. Fox, Rector of Christ Church of Jefferson County, Miss., joined in marriage Benjamin F. West and PERMELIA/PAMELA/PAULINA MENG(E),[459] daughter of George Meng(e) and Mary [—?—], of Louisville, Jefferson Co., Kentucky:[460]

> Married—On Thursday evening the 16th instant, by the Rev. James A. Fox, at the residence of John Foster, Esq., in Jefferson county, Mr. Benjamin West, to Miss Paulina Meng, of Louisville, Ky.[461]

The couple's entry in the 1830 U.S. census of Jefferson Co., Miss., includes one male under five who was likely their first child and son.[462] Indirect evidence suggests this couple may have had two sons before Permelia's death in 1833.[463]

Benjamin F. West married a second time, to his late wife's niece GABRIELLA JOHNSTON (daughter of Gabriel Johnston and Elizabeth Meng)[464] on 24 May 1836 in Jefferson County, Kentucky.[465] Their 1840 household in Claiborne County, Miss., included one male age ten to sixteen, and one female under age five;[466] they had buried their first child several months earlier.[467] Their next three children all survived to adulthood, but Benjamin died in Port Gibson, Claiborne Co., Miss., on 22 August 1845, when all his children were minors:

> Obituary
> DIED - On Friday, the 22d ult. at the residence of his brother [Charles West], in Jefferson county, of apoplexy, Benjamin F. West Esq. in the 41st year of his age.

---

[458] Ibid.

[459] Jefferson Co., Miss., Marriage Records, B:21, Benjamin F. West and Permelia Menge, 16 April 1829; FHL microfilm 893,070.

[460] *Find a Grave* (www.findagrave.com), Paulina M. West, 1 November 1833, memorial 56369853, by William Sanders; photographs (Wintergreen Cemetery, Claiborne Co., Miss.). "...youngest Daughter of George and Mary Meug of Louisville, Kentucky"; "aged 25 years 8 mo's & 13 days." Also, Joyce Shannon Bridges, *Wintergreen Cemetery, Port Gibson, Claiborne County, Mississippi* (Shreveport, La.: J & W Enterprises, n.d.), 47.

[461] *Statesman & Gazette* (Natchez, Miss.), 25 April 1829, v.3, no.17, p.3, col.4.

[462] 1830 U.S. census, Jefferson Co., Miss., p.35 stamped, p.199 written, 17th name from top, B. F. West household; NARA microfilm M19, roll 71.

[463] *Find a Grave* (www.findagrave.com), Thomas Franklin West, 27 August 1834, memorial 56370187, by William Sanders; photographs (Wintergreen Cemetery, Claiborne Co., Miss.). "...aged 15 mo.s and 4 days." Bridges, *Wintergreen Cemetery*, 47. Benjamin's probate records document that he left a son John F. West, whose position as first in the list of minor children suggests he was born to Benjamin's first wife.

[464] Jefferson Co., Ky., Marriage bond and certification, Gabriel Johnston and Elizabeth Meng, 26 June 1815; FHL microfilm 817,862. Jefferson Co., Ky., Marriage bond and certification, Benjamin F. West and Gabriella Johnston, 24 May 1836, with father Gabriel J. Johnston's consent, 24 May 1836; FHL microfilm 817,874.

[465] Jefferson Co., Ky., Marriage bond and certification, West-Johnston, 1836.

[466] 1840 U.S. census, Miss., Claiborne Co., Miss., p.72, 10th name from bottom of page, Benj. F. West household; NARA microfilm M704, roll 213.

[467] *Find a Grave* (www.findagrave.com), Walter Cato West, 25 November 1839, memorial 56370371, by William Sanders; photograph (Wintergreen Cemetery, Claiborne Co., Miss.). "Son of Benjamin F. & Gabriela I. West...aged 2 years, 4 months, & 23 days." Also, Bridges, *Wintergreen Cemetery*, 47.

The deceased was a native of Jefferson, but has long resided in this county, where his moral worth and excellence made him many warm friends, who now sincerely deplore his loss.

For several years past he has been subject to apoplectic attacks, which have rendered his life precarious, but previous to the last violent attack which resulted in his death, his health seemed to have somewhat improved.

Yet though thus suddenly cut off, he was not unprepared, for having embraced the christian religion in all humility and faith, he terminated his blameless and irreproachable life upon earth, for a more blissful and eternal home. Leaving to his bereaved and affectionate wife and children, the blessed assurance that his undying spirit had mounted upward to Heaven, there, amid saints and angels, and the redeemed of Earth, to await their coming.[468]

The widowed Gabriella (Johnston) West remarried in Claiborne County on 9 May 1849,[469] to Marmaduke Tilden of Maryland.[470] The couple had three children before Marmaduke died, on 15 January 1855.[471] The only one of the three children to survive to adulthood, Belle, and her mother removed to Mobile, Alabama, by 1880,[472] and were yet residing there in 1900, at which time the census recorded Belle as a musician who played the organ.[473]

Gabriella outlived her second husband by more than 50 years:

Death of a [F]ormer Port Gibson Lady
Mrs. Gabriella J. Tilden died at Mobile last Sunday and the remains were brought to Port Gibson, her former home, and interred Tuesday.
Mrs. Tilden was born in Kentucky 92 years ago next August, most of her girlhood being spent in Louisville. When still a young lady she came to Claiborne county on a visit and married Mr. Benjamin West. Four children by this marriage lived to be grown. After Mr. West's death she married Marmaduke Tilden. During her marriage with him she lived about 9 miles south of Port Gibson on Woodbine plantation. He died in 1855. During the civil war Mrs. Tilden's residence was burned and she went to the neighborhood of Fayette and spent the time with relatives of her first husband. About 1869 she came to Port Gibson and resided here five or six years, when she moved to Mobile, Ala. She joined the Methodist church in early life, and was a faithful member up to the time of her death.
Two daughters survive her, Mrs. Eli Jones of Harriston, Miss., and Miss Belle Tilden of Mobile, Ala., besides a number of grandchildren and great-grandchildren.
Rev. W. H. Harris condu[cte]d the service. The pall bearers were as follows:

---

[468] Obituary, *Port-Gibson Herald* (Port Gibson, Miss.), 4 September 1845, p.2, MDAH microfilm 29636.
[469] *Port Gibson Herald and Correspondent* (Port Gibson, Miss.), v.7, no.37, p.3, col.1, 11 May 1849: "Married on Wednesday evening last, the 9th inst., by the Rev. Thos. B. Adams, Mr. M. D. Tilden to Mrs. Gabriella J. West."
[470] 1850 U.S. census, Claiborne Co., Miss., Dist. 2, p.242 written, dwelling 293, family 290, M.D. Tilden household; NARA microfilm M432, roll 370.
[471] Bridges, *Wintergreen Cemetery*, p.47: Marmaduke Tilden Jr. (b. 23 July 1851—d. 19 April 1852); Belle Tevis Tilden (d. 11 February 1942), and Emily McIntyre Tilden (b. 18 May 1855—d. 18 Oct 1859).
[472] 1880 U.S. census, Mobile Co., Ala., Mobile, Ward 1, ED 130, p.51 written, p.225 stamped, dwelling 440, family 581, in Bartholomew Labuzan household; NARA microfilm T9, roll 25.
[473] 1900 U.S. census, Mobile Co., Ala., Mobile Ward 7 ED 107, p.9B, 401 St. Louis St., dwelling 166, family 213, Gabriella Tilden household; NARA microfilm T623, roll 32.

J. B. Allen, A. K. Brashear, Maurice Cahn, J. T. Drake, H. W. M. Drake, H. C. Mounger, M. M. Satterfield, and C. R. Wharton.[474]

The children of Benjamin Franklin[4] West and Permelia/Pamela/Paulina Meng(e):

    i.   JOHN FOSTER[5] WEST, b. August 1830;[475] married Mrs. Athens (Bullen) Scott;[476] d. 3 November 1904.[477] No known issue.

    ii.   THOMAS FRANKLIN WEST, b. May 1833; d. August 1834.[478]

The children of Benjamin Franklin[4] West and Gabriella Johnston:[479]

    i.   WALTER ADRIAN CATO[5] WEST, b. 2 July 1837; d. 25 November 1839.[480]

    ii.   LAURA OCTAVIA WEST, b. ca. 1839; married Gen. Thomas P. Dockery[481]; d. 8 September 1880.[482] Children: *(a)* Nydia E., April 1860-19 February 1911,[483] married Richard Howell Forman[484]; *(b)* Octavia, 1865-22 April 1949.[485]

    iii.   GABRIEL JOHNSTON WEST, b. ca. 1841; married (1) Juliet A. Dixon,

---

[474] *Port Gibson Reveille* (Port Gibson, Miss.), 30 January 1908, new series v.32, no.40, p.1, col.1, obituary of Gabriella Tilden. Another detailed obituary identifies her siblings: *Natchez Democrat* (Natchez, Miss.), 30 January 1908, new series v.36, no.52, p.2, col.1.

[475] 1900 U.S. census, Jefferson Co., Miss., Beat 4, ED 88, p.5A, dwelling 93, family 102; John F. West household; NARA microfilm T623, roll 812.

[476] Jefferson Co., Miss., Marriage Records, Book B:21, 1904, West-Scott; FHL microfilm 893,070.

[477] "United States Headstone Applications for U.S. Military Veterans, 1925-1949," database with images, *FamilySearch* (https://familysearch.org/ark:/61903/1:1:VHZN-4BD : 12 March 2018), John Foster West; citing NARA RG 92, microfilm M1916. The applicant, Mrs. M. A. Coffey, was Mary "Mamie" A. West (who married John M. Coffey in 1872), the daughter of John Foster West's younger half-brother Gabriel West.

[478] *Find a Grave* (www.findagrave.com), Thomas Franklin West, (27?) August 1834, memorial 56370187, by William Sanders; photograph (Wintergreen Cemetery, Claiborne Co., Miss.). Age at death 15 months and 4 days.

[479] 1850 U.S. census, Claiborne Co., Miss., Dist. 2, p.121B stamped, 242 written, dwelling 293, family 290, M. D. Tilden household; NARA microfilm M432, roll 370.

[480] *Natchez Weekly Courier* (Natchez, Miss.), 21 December 1839, v.11, no.46, p.3, col.5, at Port Gibson. *Find a Grave* (www.findagrave.com), Walter Cato West, 25 November 1839, memorial 56370371, by William Sanders; photograph (Wintergreen Cemetery, Claiborne Co., Miss.). "Son of Benjamin F. & Gabriela I. West...aged 2 years, 4 months, & 23 days."

[481] *FamilySearch* (www.familysearch.org), "Mississippi Marriages, 1800-1911," database, Thomas P. Dockery and Laura A. West, 16 June 1859; citing Claiborne [County], Mississippi; FHL microfilm 875,443.

[482] *Arkansas Democrat* (Little Rock, Ark.), 15 September 1880, v.7, no.35, p.4, col. 2, "Local Brevities," citing the *Helena Yeoman*, obituary of Mrs. Gen.Thos. P. Dockery, "who died at the residence of Esq. Mask, Coahoma County, Mississippi, on Wednesday last."

[483] 1900 U.S. census, Adams Co., Miss., Natchez, Part of Beat 1, ED 9, p.6B written, dwelling no. crossed out, family 145, R. H. Forman household; Nydia born April 1860; NARA microfilm T623, roll 799. *Find a Grave* (www.findagrave.com), Nydia Dockery Forman, 1860-1911, memorial 69960642 by Charles Walthall; photograph of modern gravestone (Natchez City Cemetery, Natchez, Miss.)

[484] *FamilySearch* (www.familysearch.org), "New York, New York City Marriage Records, 1829-1940," database, Richard Forman and "Lydia" Dockery, 18 January 1888; citing Marriage, Manhattan, New York, New York, United States, New York City Municipal Archives, New York; FHL microfilm 1,556,989.

[485] 1870 U.S. census, Columbia Co., Arkansas, Warren Twp., p.2 written, follows stamped p.469, dwelling and family 11, Thomas P. Dockery household; NARA microfilm M593, roll 50. *Find a Grave* (www.findagrave.com), Octavia Dockery, 22 April 1949, "Mistress of Goat Castle," memorial 32238781 by Michelle Woodham; photograph (Natchez City Cemetery, Natchez, Miss.).

28 September 1865[486]; d. 26 July 1907.[487] Children: *(a)* Leila M., b.ca.1867; *(b)* Robert E., b.ca.1869; *(c)* Benjamin F. or J., b.ca.1870; *(d)* Thomas D., b.ca.1871; *(e)* Mary A., b.ca.1874; *(f)* Gabriel J., b.ca.1876.[488] Married (2) Lizzie (Scott) Drake, 27 March 1892.[489]

iv.   BENJAMIN F. WEST, JR., b. 27 February 1843; d. 17 February 1872.[490]

v.   MARY MCL. WEST, b. 1844; married Ely Ross Jones, 23 October 1868;[491] died 1926.[492] Children[493]: *(a)* John G., b.ca.1869; *(b)* Benny W., b.ca.1871; *(c)* Ely Ross, Jr., b.ca.1873; *(d)* Laura Belle, b.ca.1879; *(e)* Mary Louisa, b. March 1886.[494]

Children of Cato West and Martha Harper

16. MARTHA ELIZABETH[4] WEST (Cato[3], William[2,1]), daughter of Cato West and Martha Harper,[495] was born in December 1812 in Jefferson Co., Miss.,[496] the first child born to Cato West's second wife, Martha Harper. Martha Elizabeth would outlive all three of her younger siblings and was only six years old when her father died. Her mother remarried a year after Cato's death,[497] and, on 23 January 1821, the Jefferson County court appointed her stepfather William L. Davis and

---

[486] *FamilySearch* (www.familysearch.org), "Mississippi Marriages, 1800-1911," database, Gabriel J. West and Juliet A. Dixon, 28 September 1865; citing Jefferson County, Mississippi; FHL microfilm 893,071 (*Ancestry* database gives "1863"). *Vicksburg Herald* (Vicksburg, Miss.), 2 November 1877, vol.14, no.263, p.3, col.4: "Of congestion at Spring Vale near Church Hill, Jefferson County, 22nd October, Mrs. Juliet A. West, wife of Capt. G. J. West. She was about 30 years old and left a husband and six young children."

[487] Brown, *Jefferson Co., Miss., Cemeteries, Etc.*, 2:99.

[488] Approximate ages for all children from the 1880 U.S. census, Jefferson Co., Miss., Beat 4, ED 63, p.2 written, follows stamped p.245, dwelling 14, family 13, G. J. West household; NARA microfilm T9, roll 651.

[489] *FamilySearch* (www.familysearch.org), "Mississippi Marriages, 1800-1911," database, Gabe J. West and L. V. Drake, 27 March 1892; citing Jefferson County, Mississippi; FHL microfilm 893,073.

[490] *Find a Grave* (www.findagrave), memorial 130819995, Benj. F. West, MD, 17 February 1872, by William Sanders; photograph (Wintergreen Cemetery, Claiborne Co., Miss.). Born 27 February 1843.

[491] *FamilySearch* (www.familysearch.org), "Mississippi Marriages, 1800-1911," database, Ely R. Jones and Mary L. West, 23 October 1868; citing Jefferson County, Mississippi; FHL microfilm 893,071.

[492] *Find a Grave* (www.findagrave), memorial 56370550, Mary Jones, 1844-1926, by William Sanders; photograph (Wintergreen Cemetery, Claiborne Co., Miss.).

[493] Data for the first four children from the 1880 U.S. census, Jefferson Co., Miss., Fayette Pct., p.219 stamped, p.33 written, dwelling 331, family 321; Eli R. Jones household; NARA microfilm T9, roll 651.

[494] 1900 U.S. census, Jefferson Co., Miss., Beat 3, ED 84, p.1B, dwelling and family 23, Eli R. Jones household; NARA microfilm T623, roll 812.

[495] Jefferson Co., Miss., Will Book A:24-25, will of Cato West names "Martha Elizabeth" West as one of his six youngest children. This is the first child born to Cato's second wife; "Married," *Raleigh Register and North-Carolina (State) Gazette* (Raleigh, N.C.), 16 August 1810, v.11, no.569, p.3, col.4: "In Jefferson County, M.T. on the 12th inst. Col. Cato West, to Miss Patsey Harper."

[496] Brown, *Jefferson Co., Miss., Cemeteries, Etc.*, 2:99: Fayette Cemetery, gives her age at death as 32 years and 6 months. Jefferson Co., Miss., Chancery Court, probate packet A-93, Jesse Harper; FHL microfilm1,888,885: "Martha Elizabeth aged 11 years. 3 years of five she has been at home[;] from her father's death up to this time [about January 1824]."

[497] Jefferson Co., Miss., Marriage Licenses and Certificates, vol. A:154: William L. Davis and Mrs. Martha West, 1820; FHL microfilm 893,070.

mother Martha (Harper) West Davis as the guardians of the estate due her under her father's will.[498]

The Chancery Court packets containing signed receipts and William Davis's yearly accounts for Martha Elizabeth's estate yield much detail about this young girl's life: Prunella shoes, fancy silk handkerchiefs, Irish linen, hair combs, a silver thimble, dancing lessons, and schooling in nearby Washington, Adams County.[499] Physician J. W. Monett filed one receipt for attending and providing medicine to Martha Elizabeth while she was at "the Academy."[500] Martha's share of Cato West's estate included six slaves—George, Harry, Mary Ann, Perry, Tamar, and Phillis— and two horses,[501] all of which Davis turned over to Martha's husband the year Martha Elizabeth married, when she was sixteen years old.[502]

Martha Elizabeth West married JAMES JEFFERSON MONTGOMERY (son of Alexander Montgomery and Lydia Swayze)[503] on 11 March 1829 in Jefferson Co., Miss.[504] The memoirs of their only known child, Frank Alexander Montgomery, describe his parents and childhood:

> From the south boundary line of what is now Claiborne county, to Natchez, I know every hill and spring and stream, for twenty-five years of my life, the days of my youth, were spent midway between Natchez and Port Gibson, and memory often takes me back to those scenes of my youth. But if I dwell too long on these things I will never tell my story.
>
> While [I was] still an infant my father moved into Jefferson county, and soon after died. He was James Jefferson Montgomery, son of Alexander Montgomery, one of the pioneer settlers of the territory, of whom Claiborne[,] in his history of Mississippi, makes honorable mention as one of the leading citizens of the territory and of the state till his death, a few years after its admission into the Union. My mother was the youngest [*sic*] daughter of Colonel Cato West, also a pioneer, who became secretary of the territory under Governor Claiborne, and for some time the acting governor when Claiborne went to New Orleans as governor of the newly-acquired territory of Louisiana.
>
> Colonel West was an intimate acquaintance and friend of General Jackson, and I have now in my possession a long autograph letter written to him by General Jackson in the year 1801, devoted to personal matters and politics, and directed to "Colonel Cato West,

---

[498] Jefferson Co., Miss., Chancery Court, probate packet B-96, Martha E. West, guardian's bond, 23 January 1821; FHL microfilm 1,889,020. Guardianship bonds for siblings Mary Louisa West and William H. West do not include their mother Martha (Harper) West as a guardian.

[499] Ibid.

[500] Ibid. Receipt no. 4, 8 October 1828.

[501] Ibid. Inventory, 28 February 1826.

[502] Ibid. Receipt no.10, 18 December 1829.

[503] *FamilySearch* (www.familysearch.org), "Mississippi Probate Records, 1781-1930," digital images, Adams County, Probate packets 1805-1841 box 24-25, Probate Court box 25, "Montgomery, Jefferson [&] Prosper," images 1617-1618, expenses starting in 1816, "John Snodgrass guardian to Jefferson & Prosper heirs of A. Montgomery"; also FHL microfilm 1,769,784. Adams Co., Miss., Marriages 1802-1819, John Snodgrass and Lydia Montgomery, 3 May 1814; FHL microfilm 893,521. Adams Co., Miss., Deed Book M:215-216, John Snodgrass and wife to Gabriel Swayze, 6 December 1820, "…formerly owned by the late Richard Swayze and by him in his lifetime allotted and laid off to his daughter Lydia (now Lydia Snodgrass)"; FHL microfilm 892,055.

[504] Jefferson Co., Miss., Marriage Records, Book B:22, Jefferson Montgomery and Martha E. West, 11 March 1829; FHL microfilm 893,070. Married by William Montgomery.

Coles Creek, Mississippi Territory." After my father's death, my mother went to live on our place on Coles creek, about two miles from Uniontown, which was at the time still a little village, and not far from the Maryland settlement, so called because some of the earliest settlers were from Maryland. The old highway spoken of ran through our place. Here after some years my mother married a Mr. Malloy, a Presbyterian minister, but she died while still a young woman, and the plantation and negroes then fell to me. In my early boyhood, and while she lived, I spent much of my time with my uncle Charles West, near Fayette, in Jefferson county, and went to school to a Mr. Roland, a Welshman, who certainly did not spare the rod, or rather the ferule, which was his favorite instrument of torture. That was the rule in those days; all teachers whipped their scholars, and indeed parents all approved it. We live now in a better day, for the best teachers rarely, if ever, resort to corporal punishment, which only tends to degrade a child and harden him.[505]

Jefferson Montgomery died before 28 October 1834, when Martha Elizabeth (West) Montgomery remarried, to ROBERT MALLOY, in Jefferson Co., Miss.[506] Census information indicates that Robert Malloy was born about 1800-1805 in North Carolina, Alabama, or Tennessee.[507] Frank Montgomery's description of Malloy as a Presbyterian minister is documented, even though the enumerator of the 1860 U.S. census recorded him as a Methodist minister.[508]

Robert Malloy signed the receipt in 1835 for his wife Martha Elizabeth's distributive share of $2,376.15 from her late sister Mary Louisa West's estate.[509] In 1840, the federal census reflects the three daughters born to Robert and Martha Elizabeth, and the 44 slaves attributed to them may be those mentioned by Frank Montgomery as belonging to the estate of his father.[510] Robert Malloy obtained patents for four tracts of Jefferson County land in 1840-1841.[511] In 1844, one of their three daughters died, and Martha Elizabeth (West) Montgomery Malloy died on 27 May 1845.[512]

In 1850, Robert Malloy was in transit. On 24 June, he was enumerated in the household of Thomas Reed and wife Lavenia West (the daughter of Charles West, with whom Robert's step-

---

[505] Frank Alexander Montgomery, *Reminiscences of a Mississippian in Peace and War* (Cincinnati: The Robert Clarke Company Press, 1901), 5-6.

[506] Jefferson Co., Miss., Marriage Records, Book B:85, Malloy-Montgomery, 28 October 1834, married by B. M. Drake; FHL microfilm 893,070. Also F. A. Montgomery's *Reminiscences*. No tombstone has been located for Jefferson Montgomery.

[507] His 1850 and 1860 U.S. census entries; his daughter's entry in the 1880 U.S. census, Copiah Co., Miss., Crystal Springs, ED 25, p.20 written, follows p.238 stamped, dwelling 178, family 185, Jane Harper household; NARA microfilm T9, roll 646.

[508] F. A. Montgomery's *Reminiscences*; extracts from the minutes of the Cumberland Synod (http://www.cumberland.org/hfcpc/minister/MolloyRobert.htm); and the 1860 U.S. census, East Baton Rouge Parish, La., p.161 written, follows p.607 written, dwelling and family 1189, Robert Malloy household; NARA microfilm M653, roll 408.

[509] Jefferson Co., Miss., Chancery Court, probate packet B-95, Mary L. West; FHL microfilm 1,889,020.

[510] 1840 U.S. census, Jefferson Co., Miss., p.290 stamped, first line: Robert Mallay; NARA microfilm 704, roll 214.

[511] U.S. Bureau of Land Management, "Land Patent Search," indexed database, *General Land Office Records* (http://glorecords.blm.gov), entries for Robert Malloy of Hinds and Jefferson Counties, Mississippi, issued 1840-1841, certificates no. 15364, 23692, 27542, and 27543.

[512] Brown, *Jefferson Co., Miss., Cemeteries, Etc.*, 2:99: Fayette Cemetery. Not in *Find a Grave* in 2019.

son Frank Montgomery often spent time) in Natchez,[513] where his two daughters were attending Rev. Samuel W. Speers's female college.[514] By 1 August 1850, Robert appeared south of the state line in West Feliciana Parish, Louisiana, where he married the widowed MARTHA OCTAVIA (WEST) DAVIS[515] (daughter of Thomas W. West and his wife, cousin Susan West). On August 23, Robert, his new wife, and her two Davis children appeared in the 1850 U.S. census of West Feliciana Parish, La.[516]

By 1860, Robert and Martha Octavia (West) Davis Malloy resided in East Baton Rouge Parish, Louisiana, where their census record included their daughter Ella.[517] Robert's second wife died there on 2 November 1867:[518]

> Died: In this city, on Saturday, the 2d inst., of yellow fever, Mrs. OCTAVIA MOLLOY, aged 53 years, a native of Jefferson County, Miss., but for several years a resident first of the interior of this parish and afterwards—during the past and present year—of this city. As a devoted wife and mother and sincere friend, Mrs. Molloy afforded enduring evidence of one whose character was thoroughly imbued with the true virtues and graces that adorn the human heart. By her bright example—conscientiously and steadfastly performing all her duties in the varied relationships of life—she well merited the honored title of Christian, and leaves to her deeply bereaved and afflicted husband and daughter the comforting assurance that she has gone to a better and happier world where an immortal crown of glory awaits her.
> "Blessed are the pure in heart, for they shall see God."[519]

Robert Malloy followed a year later. A tombstone at his final resting place in Beulah Cemetery, Bolivar County, Miss., furnished his death date as 25 November 1868.[520]

---

[513] 1850 U.S. census, Adams Co., Miss., "City of Natchez, North," p.20 stamped, p.39 written, dwelling and family 45, Thos. Reed household with Robert "Maloy"; NARA microfilm M432, roll 368.

[514] 1850 U.S. census, Adams Co., Miss., "City of Natchez, North," p.18 stamped, p.35 written, dwelling and family 11, Jane and Francis [sic] "Maloy" on lines 32-33. Charles Force Deems, *Annals of Southern Methodism for 1856* (Nashville: Stevenson & Owen, 1857), 2:138.

[515] West Feliciana Parish, La., Marriages, A:182-183, Malloy-Davis, 1 August 1860; FHL microfilm 364,651. Robert's first bride was Cato West's daughter. Robert's second bride was both Cato West's granddaughter (Martha Octavia[4], Susan[3], Cato[2], William[1]) as well as Cato's great-niece (Martha Octavia[4] West, Thomas W.[3], Charles[2], William[1]).

[516] 1850 U.S. census, West Feliciana Par., La., p.272B stamped, p.544 written, dwelling 335, family 340, Robt. Maloy in Thomas Reed household; NARA microfilm M432, roll 231.

[517] 1860 U.S. census, East Baton Rouge Par., La., p.161 written, follows written p.607, dwelling and family 1189, Robert Malloy household, including Ella age 9; NARA microfilm M653, roll 408.

[518] *Weekly Gazette and Comet* (Baton Rouge, La.), Saturday, 9 November 1867, v.49, no.45, p.3, col.2 (photocopy courtesy of Candance Bundgard).

[519] Ibid.

[520] *Find a Grave* (www.findagrave.com), Robert Malloy, 25 November 1868, memorial 14182223 by "NatalieMaynor"; photograph (Beulah Cemetery, Beulah, Bolivar County, Miss.). Died at age 68 years.

The known child of Martha Elizabeth[4] West and James Jefferson Montgomery:

      i.   FRANK ALEXANDER[5] MONTGOMERY, b. 7 January 1830; married Charlotte Clark on 12 January 1848;[521] died 16 December 1903.[522] Children: *(a)* Louisiana "Loulie," 26 April 1849-19 April 1868[523]; *(b)* James Jefferson, 3 December 1850-17 April 1921[524]; *(c)* Matilda Sillers, b.August 1852-17 July 1928[525]; *(d)* Martha, 1854-1944;[526] *(e)* Harriet, b.ca.1856[527]; *(f)* Franklin Alexander, 23 September 1858-12 June 1922[528]; *(g)* Charlotte, b. April 1861[529]; *(h)* Frances "Fadgie," b.February 1866-8 May 1935[530]; *(i)* Joseph Sillers, 29 November 1868-15 August 1894[531]; and *(j)* Annie, 1871-1961.[532]

---

[521] Jefferson Co., Miss., Marriage Book B:231, Montgomery-Clark, 12 January 1848; FHL microfilm 893,070.

[522] *Find a Grave* (www.findagrave.com), Col. Frank A. Montgomery, 16 December 1903, memorial 5990256 but no creator's name; photograph added by Gene Phillips (Beulah Cemetery, Bolivar County, Miss.). Born "7 Jan 1830."

[523] *Find a Grave* (www.findagrave.com), Loulie Montgomery, 19 April 1868, memorial 45018810 by A. I. Zimmer; no photograph (Beulah Cemetery, Bolivar Co., Miss.). 1860 U.S. census, Bolivar Co., Miss., p.30 and p.530 written, dwelling 318, family 202, household of F. A. Montgomery, with Louisiana age eleven; NARA microfilm M653, roll 578.

[524] *Find a Grave* (www.findagrave.com), J. J. Montgomery, 17 April 1921, memorial 14182238, by "NatalieMaynor"; photograph (Beulah Cemetery, Bolivar Co., Miss.). Born 3 December 1850. 1860 U.S. census, Bolivar Co., Miss., p.30 and p.530 written, dwelling 318, family 202, household of F. A. Montgomery, with James Jefferson age nine; NARA microfilm M653, roll 578.

[525] *Find a Grave* (www.findagrave.com), Matilda Sillers Montgomery, 17 July 1828, memorial 45018833 by A. I. Zimmer; no photograph (Beulah Cemetery, Bolivar Co., Miss.). 1900 U.S. census, Bolivar Co., Miss., Beat 3, ED 10, p.2B, dwelling and family 34, household of Frank A. Montgomery, with Matilda born August 1852; NARA microfilm T623, roll 801.

[526] *Find a Grave* (www.findagrave.com), Martha Montgomery Moore, 1854, memorial 45018894 by A. I. Zimmer; photograph by Gene Phillips (Beulah Cemetery, Bolivar Co., Miss.). 1860 U.S. census, Bolivar Co., Miss., p.30 and p.530 written, dwelling 318, family 202, household of F. A. Montgomery, with Martha age six.

[527] 1860 U.S. census, Bolivar Co., Miss., p.30 and p.530 written, dwelling 318, family 202, household of F. A. Montgomery, with Harriet age four; NARA microfilm M653, roll 578. 1870 U.S. census, Bolivar Co., Miss., Range 8, p.93 written, 250A stamped, dwelling and family 780, household of Frank Montgomery, with "Hariet" age fourteen; NARA microfilm M593, roll 722.

[528] *Find a Grave* (www.findagrave.com), Frank Alexander Montgomery, 12 June 1922, memorial 26396419 by Michelle Woodham; photograph (Oakwood Cemetery, Tunica Co., Miss.).

[529] 1900 U.S. census, Bolivar Co., Miss., Beat 3, ED 10, p.2B, dwelling and family 34, household of Frank A. Montgomery, with Charlotte born April 1861; NARA microfilm T623, roll 801.

[530] "Beulah Cemetery (Part 1), Beulah, Bolivar County, Mississippi," transcription of gravestone inscriptions by Marsha Chenault for USGenWeb Archives (http://msgw.org/bolivar/beulah.pdf), image 16 of 34, Fadgie Montgomery Guice Campbell, died 8 May 1935.

[531] "Beulah Cemetery (Part 1), Beulah, Bolivar County, Mississippi," transcription of gravestone inscriptions by Marsha Chenault for USGenWeb Archives (http://msgw.org/bolivar/beulah.pdf), image 15 of 34, Joseph Sillers Montgomery, 29 November 1868-15 August 1894.

[532] "Beulah Cemetery (Part 1), Beulah, Bolivar County, Mississippi," transcription of gravestone inscriptions by Marsha Chenault for USGenWeb Archives (http://msgw.org/bolivar/beulah.pdf), image 16 of 34, Annie Montgomery Hull, 1871-1951.

The known children of Martha Elizabeth[4] West and Robert Malloy:

    i.   JANE ELIZABETH[5] MALLOY, b. 12 September 1835; married James P. Harper of West Feliciana Parish on 30 July 1856;[533] d. 23 August 1921.[534] Children: *(a)* Mattie W., b.ca.1857-17 November 1868[535]; *(b)* Mary Roberta, 30 September 1862-4 March 1942[536]; and *(c)* James P., b.ca.1867.[537]

    ii.   FRANCES MALLOY, b. ca. 1838; d. after 1860.[538]

    iii.   EMILY WEST MALLOY, b. 1838; d. 3 September 1844.[539]

17. MARY LOUISA[4] WEST (*Cato[3], William[2,1]*) was born likely about 1814 in Jefferson Co., Miss., so less than five years old at her father's death.[540] After Mary Louisa's widowed mother married William L. Davis in 1820, he took guardianship responsibility for her.[541] The voluminous receipts and annual accounts he filed give insight into her brief and privileged life. The accounts, like those for her sister, show purchases of textiles, "Morocco" shoes, and jewelry for Mary Louisa as well as spelling and "English Grammar" books,[542] and track the annual income from hiring out the slaves distributed to her (Albert, Sarah, Lucy, Hector, and Mary).[543]

Mary Louisa, who often appears in these records as "Louisa" or "Louiza," also inherited land from her late father Cato West.[544] In 1825, her guardian obtained permission from the court to sell some of her land; her estate packet included county surveyor and chain carrier accounts and receipts that corroborate the sale.[545] Although William L. Davis's accounts include reimbursements for boarding Mary Louisa, she may not have been happy with the arrangement and apparently did not stay in her remarried mother's home all the time.

---

[533] East Baton Rouge Parish, La., Marriage Record, vol. 5:634, Harper-Malloy, 1856; FHL microfilm 327,738.

[534] *Find a Grave* (www.findagrave.com), Jane Elizabeth Harper, 23 August 1921, memorial 33598843 by "timcdfw"; photograph (Arlington Cemetery, Tarrant Co., Texas). Born "12 September 1835."

[535] "Beulah Cemetery (Part 1), Beulah, Bolivar County, Mississippi," transcription of gravestone inscriptions by Marsha Chenault for USGenWeb Archives (http://msgw.org/bolivar/beulah.pdf), image 5 of 34, Mattie W. Harper, "aged 11 years."

[536] *FamilySearch* (www.familysearch.org), "Mississippi Marriages, 1800-1911," J. J. Montgomery and Roberta Harper, 14 February 1882; citing Copiah, Mississippi; FHL microfilm 876,494. *Ancestry* (www.ancestry.com), "Texas, Death Certificates, 1903-1982," Dallas>1942>Jan-Mar, image 793, Mary Montgomery, 4 March 1942, certificate 11232.

[537] 1880 U.S. census, Copiah Co., Miss., Crystal Springs, ED 25, p.20, dwelling 178, family 185, household of Jane Harper, with son James P., age thirteen; NARA microfilm T9, roll 646.

[538] 1860 U.S. census, East Baton Rouge Par., La., p.161 written, dwelling and family 1189, Robert Malloy household; NARA microfilm M653, roll 408.

[539] Brown, *Jefferson Co., Miss., Cemeteries, Etc.*, 2:99: Fayette Cemetery.

[540] Jefferson Co., Miss., Chancery Court, probate packet A-93 for Jesse Harper; FHL microfilm 1,888,885: "Mary Louisa West, 9 years old[,] has been at home all the time[;] five years" [[since her father's death in January 1819, so written about January 1824]. This supports her birth after January 1814.

[541] Jefferson Co., Miss., Chancery Court, probate packet B-95, Mary L. West; FHL microfilm 1,889,020. Davis appointed guardian of Mary Louisa West on 23 January 1821.

[542] Ibid., itemized 1831 bill from John W. and Levi Pipes, 28 February 1832.

[543] Ibid., inventory of estate, 1 February 1825. The 1832 final guardianship account shows Davis charged Mary Louisa's account for maintaining three young male slaves (presumably the children of the named adults distributed to her): Jacob for 4 years, "Jef." for 3 years, and Alex for 3 years.

[544] Ibid.

[545] Ibid., 1825, Duncan Currie, county surveyor; 1826, Ephraim Lu[?]y, chain carrier.

She also did not appear to be pleased with her stepfather's handling of her inheritance. On 23 December 1832, "M. Louisa West" signed a petition—addressed to Philip Dixon, Judge of Probate—stating that "she is a minor over the age of fourteen years & no testamentary or other guardian was appointed for her by her deceased Father Cato West, [and] she therefore prays that your Honor would appoint Mr. Charles West her guardian."[546] A local J.P. certified that she appeared before him on 24 December 1832 to acknowledge the petition as hers.[547]

On that same date, Dr. S. P. French tended to Mary Louisa at her half-brother Charles West's home, according to his bill.[548] This may have been the beginning of her final illness, as the doctor's bill shows that he last made a house call to treat Mary Louisa shortly thereafter, on 10 January 1833, at which time she was at her sister's house: "To visit at Mrs. Montgomery at Coles Creek (11 M[iles]), $11.00...sundry medicines &c, $2.00."[549]

Mr. A. Hamberlin's $35.00 charge for "a Sup[r] Coffin" was paid by 26 January 1833.[550] On 15 May 1833, guardian William L. Davis advertised that he would present his final account as "Guardian of the Estate of the late Mary L. West" for settlement and allowance at the June term of the Orphans Court.[551] Mary Louisa West was not yet age twenty when she died in mid-January 1833 and she was likely buried in the family cemetery mentioned in her father Cato West's last will and testament.[552]

18. CATO[4] WEST JR. (*Cato[3], William[2,1]*), son of Cato West and Martha Harper,[553] was born about 1816 in Jefferson Co., Miss.[554] When Cato Jr. was about two years old, Cato Sr. made his last will and testament in which Cato Jr. was to receive the part of the plantation on which Cato Sr. then lived, along with other specified land.[555] Both Cato Sr. and Jr. died within two years of each other, and estate records for each of them appear filed in one Chancery Court packet labeled solely as "Cato West Jr."[556]

On 23 January 1821, William L. Davis signed bonds to serve as administrator of the estate of Cato West Jr. and as guardian for the late Cato Jr.'s siblings Martha, Mary, and William (all children from Cato West Sr.'s second marriage and, by 1821, all Davis's stepchildren).[557]

---

[546] Ibid., 1832, M. Louisa West's guardian request.

[547] Ibid., 1832, J.P.'s certificate on reverse side.

[548] Ibid., 1832, Dr. French's claim.

[549] Ibid.

[550] Ibid., 1833 Hamberlin's receipt acknowledging payment. However, a similar charge appears on the "No. 8, account current," dated 20 May 1832.

[551] *Port-Gibson correspondent, and Mississippi general advertiser* (Port Gibson, Miss.), 1 June 1833, v.14, no.31, p.5, col. 1, "Notice."

[552] Jefferson Co., Miss., Will Book A:24-25, will of Cato West, 30 July 1818.

[553] Ibid.; will of Cato West lists "Cato" West last among his six youngest children.

[554] Estimate based on three known pregnancies following the December 1812 birth of Cato West and Martha Harper's first child Martha Elizabeth and the August 1818 creation of Cato West's last will and testament.

[555] Jefferson Co., Miss., Will Book A:24-25, will of Cato West.

[556] Jefferson Co., Miss., Chancery Court, probate packet B-98, Cato West Jr.; FHL microfilm 1,889,020. Estate records pertaining to various children of Cato West Sr. appear in Chancery Court packets other than their own.

[557] Jefferson Co., Miss., Chancery Court, probate packet B-96, Martha West, includes 23 January 1821 guardian's bond; FHL microfilm 1,889,020. See also Jefferson Co., Miss., Orphans Court Minutes 1814-1822, 197, January 1821; FHL microfilm 1,939,843.

Receipts found within the combined Cato West packet provide evidence that places the death of Cato West Jr. between 13 and 15 November 1820:

```
1820
Nov 13th       To attendance & medicine      55.00
...            McConnell & Duncan[558]


Wm. L. Davis in Acct with Anth. Hamberlin
1820
Novembr 15th  To 1 Coffin for Child          18.00
Decembr 18    " dressing four Tables
              @ 3.50 Each is                  14.00
                                             32.00[559]
```

Another probate record provides additional information on Cato Jr.—and on the death date of his father Cato Sr.—even though it is undated, unsigned, and appears filed in the probate packet for his maternal grandfather, Jesse Harper.[560] A receipt for "[t]he Estate of Colo. Cato West dec'd, in a/c to Wm. L. Davis for board," lists, among others, some of Cato's children. One entry reads, "Cato Jun'r Dec'd, one year & ten months from his father's death to his[;] 4 years old." This information supports a November 1816 birth date for Cato West Jr., and supports a January 1819 death date for his father, as the doctor's bill for Cato West Sr. suggested.

Cato West Jr. was likely buried in the family cemetery mentioned in his father Cato West's last will and testament.[561]

19. WILLIAM H.[4] WEST (*Cato³, William².¹*), son of Cato West and Martha Harper,[562] was born likely on 7 February 1819 in Jefferson Co., Miss.[563] William's birth date suggests he was Cato's posthumous child, and William's stepfather William L. Davis later confirmed this in an undated list of boarding costs he was due: "William West, Dec'd, an infant three years old when he died[;] *born after his father's death*" [emphasis added].[564]

The Chancery Court packet bearing William H. West's name contains the 23 January 1821 bond for William L. Davis to serve as guardian of stepson William H. West's share of Cato West's estate.[565] However, the packet contains no inventories, claims, receipts, or accounts but rather a

---

[558] Jefferson Co., Miss., Chancery Court, probate packet B-98, Cato West Jr.
[559] Ibid.
[560] Jefferson Co., Miss., Chancery Court, probate packet A-93, Jesse Harper; FHL microfilm 1,888,885.
[561] Jefferson Co., Miss., Will Book A:24-25, will of Cato West, 30 July 1818.
[562] Jefferson Co., Miss., Chancery Court, probate packet B-98, estate of Cato West Jr.[*sic*]; expenses for William H. West, minor (including his burial), charged to the estate of Cato West.
[563] Cato West's 30 July 1818 will refers to the fact that his wife was then pregnant (Jefferson Co., Miss., Will Book A:24), and the doctor's claim against Cato West's estate included a detailed statement that showed he prescribed laudanum on 7 February 1819 (Jefferson Co., Miss., Chancery Court, probate packet B-98, Cato West Jr. [*sic*]; FHL microfilm 1,889,020).
[564] Jefferson Co., Miss., Chancery Court, probate packet A-93, Jesse Harper, FHL microfilm 1,888,885.
[565] Jefferson Co., Miss., Chancery Court, probate packet B-93, William H. West; FHL microfilm 1,889,020.

series of court summonses, trying to get William L. Davis to appear and settle the account. The 31 May 1826 summons document is the first to refer to William H. West as deceased.[566]

The probate packet for "Cato West Jr." contains additional receipts and accounts for William H. West that show he died much earlier than 1826.[567] Dr. Duncan and carpenter Henry Siebe submitted claims in early 1822 against the estate of "Wm. West (minor) dec'd,"[568] the payments of which point to William's approximate death date:

> [No. 18]
> Received 16th February 1822 of William L. Davis ten dollars in full of a Medical act for
> little William West.   John F. Duncan.[569]

> [No. 19]
> To Wm. L. Davis
> to a raised lid chery [sic] coffin and trimend [?]   —20.00
> to a large poplar Do   ——12.00
> $32.00
>
> Received the above above [sic] in ful[l]
> January the 16 1822   Henry Siebe[570]

A modest receipt, for one dollar, appears to pinpoint William's death date further:

> [No. 20]
> 1821 Decr 3 To cash paid for one Velvet Ribbond [sic] to put on to Coffin.
> Recd payment per Mr. W. Gillaspie.
>   Wm. Crommelin[571]

The list that William West's stepfather drafted, of boarding costs for the late Cato West's children, casts uncertainty about whether the coffin ribbon pertained to William West's coffin, in that Davis stated William died when he was "three years old."[572] The estimate of William's posthumous birth on or about 7 February 1819, and death before 3 December 1822 would make him just shy of two years and ten months old at death. The Davis list does, however, confirm that William was a posthumous child and William's own probate records (found in Cato West Jr.'s probate packet) document his death before 16 January 1822, when William would not have reached his third birthday.

William H. West was likely buried in the family cemetery mentioned in his father Cato West's last will and testament.[573]

---

[566] Ibid., 31 May 1826 summons.
[567] Jefferson Co., Miss., Chancery Court, probate packet B-98, Cato West Jr. [sic]; FHL microfilm 1,889,020.
[568] Ibid., 22 January 1822.
[569] Ibid., Dr. Duncan's receipt.
[570] Ibid., Mr. Siebe's receipt. The large poplar coffin may reflect the contemporaneous death of a slave.
[571] Ibid., Mr. Crommelin's receipt.
[572] Jefferson Co., Miss., Chancery Court, probate packet A-93, Jesse Harper.
[573] Jefferson Co., Miss., Will Book A:24-25, will of Cato West, 30 July 1818.

Index

Louis (enslaved by H.J. Balch 1816), 42
Lucy (enslaved by John S. West 1821), 60
Lucy (enslaved by Mary Louisa West 1825), 84
Lucy (enslaved by Wm. West 1810), 28
Mariah (enslaved by Wm. West 1769), 2
Marmada (enslaved by Cato West 1818), 17
Mary (enslaved by John S. West 1821), 60
Mary (enslaved by Mary Louisa West 1825), 84
Mary Ann (enslaved by Martha E. West 1826), 77
Melford (enslaved by Wm. West 1769), 3
Milly (enslaved by Charles West 1859), 46
Mindon? (enslaved by Wm. West 1810), 28
Nace (enslaved by Wm. West 1769), 2, 3
Nancy (enslaved by Cato West 1818), 17
Nancy (enslaved by Martha (Harper) West 1811), 16
Ned (enslaved by Wm. West 1810), 28
Olwell (enslaved by Charles West 1859), 46
Peggy (enslaved by Charles West 1859), 46
Per[?]y (enslaved by John S. West 1821), 60
Perry (enslaved by Martha E. West 1826), 77
Peter (1809) (enslaved by Thomas West 1818), 39
Peter (enslaved by Wm. West 1810), 28
Phebe (enslaved by Wm. West 1769), 3
Philis (enslaved by John S. West 1821), 60
Philis (enslaved by Wm. West 1810, 28
Phillis (enslaved by Martha E. West 1826), 77
Pug (enslaved by Wm. West 1769), 2, 3
Rhoda (enslaved by R. C. West (1825), 62
Sall (enslaved by Wm. West 1810), 28
Sally (wife of Leroy 1859), 46

Sarah (enslaved by John S. West 1821), 60
Sarah (enslaved by Mary Louisa West 1825), 84
Sarah (enslaved by Wm. West 1769), 3
Sib (enslaved by Wm. West 1769), 3
Suba? (enslaved by Wm. West 1810), 28
Sylvia (enslaved by John S. West 1821), 61
Tamar (enslaved by Martha E. West 1826), 77
Thamer (enslaved by John S. West 1821), 60
Tom (1800) (enslaved by Thomas West 1818), 39
Tom (enslaved by Wm. West 1769), 2, 3
Wat (enslaved by John S. West 1821), 61
Wat (enslaved by Joseph Winn 1826), 53
William (enslaved by Cato West 1818), 17
York (enslaved by John S. West 1821), 60
Abbey
  R., 31
  Richard (Rev.), 30
Adams
  Thomas B. (Rev.), 74
Adams Co., Miss., 14, 23, 25, 26, 35, 36, 41, 52, 75, 77, 78, 80
Alabama
  Mobile, 74
  state formation, 16
Alexander
  John, 6
Alison
  John, 3
Allen
  D. J., 68
  J. B., 74
Allison
  Robert, 11
Amite Co., Miss., 55
Arkansas
  Arkansas Co., 19
  Columbia Co., 76
  Little Rock, 75
Arkansas Co., Ark., 19

Atchison
  Elizabeth Jane, 56
  James, 56
  Martha P. (Winn), 56
  Samuel, 54, 56
  Sarah Ann, 56
Atterbury
  William, 5
Austin
  John, 23
Austin, Texas, 70
Baconfort, 2
Baker
  Elizabeth, 35, 36
  L., Esq., 37
  William, 4
Balch
  Ann, 42
  Elizabeth "Betsy" (West), 15, 20, 26, 40
  Hezekiah J., Dr., 16, 20, 26, 40
  Hezekiah Sr., 40
  Martha (McCandless), 40, 41
  Mary (West), 22, 26, 41
Bank of the State of Miss., 59
Barland
  William, 12
Barnes
  Henry W., 25
Baton Rouge, La., 80
Bayly
  Peirce, 8
Bean
  William, 11
Benavides
  Plácido, 64
Bennett
  John, 64
Betzell
  Isaac, 2
Beulah Cemetery, Miss., 81
Bexar Co., Texas, 66
Binns
  C., Co. Clerk, 5
Black Hawk, Miss., 55, 56
Bolivar Co., Miss., 55, 82
  Beulah Cemetery, 81

Bonner
  Mattie M. (Dixon), 50
Boston, Mass., 29, 31
Boyce
  Robert, 42
Bradley Co., Tenn., 10
Brashear(s)
  A. K., 74
  Delilah, 63
  Susannah (Vaughan), 63
  Zadoc, 63
Brevard
  Elizabeth Mary, 32
  Robert, 34
Brown
  Lt. Col., 9
Bull Run, 2
Bullen
  Athens, 75
  Benjamin, Dr., 18, 38, 39
Bullock
  R., 37
Cahn
  Maurice, 74
Caldwell
  Ann (Balch), 42
  Samuel S., 42
Calhoun Co., Texas, 65, 66, 67, 69, 71
Calvit
  Thomas, 38, 43
Camden District, S.C., 9
Caraway
  Vestal, 63
Carradine
  Parker, 23
Carroll Co., Miss., 55, 56, 57
Carter
  Robert, 2
Catahoula Parish, La., 27, 28
Chance
  Capt., 26
Chaney
  Betsy, 23
Charleston, S.C., 10
Cherokee Bower, Miss. or La., 48
Chester Co., S.C., 10

Catahoula Par., 27, 28
East Baton Rouge Par., 79, 80, 83
Harrisonburg, 31
Militia 1815, 26
New Orleans, 25, 26, 38, 66, 78
Plaquemine, 25
Pointe Coupee Par., 25
Sicily Island, 29
Waterproof, 68
West Feliciana Par., 23, 24, 51, 80, 83
Louisville, Ky., 72, 74
Lu[?]y
Ephraim, 84
Mackey
Walter, 39
Madison
James, 15
Madison Co., Miss., 49
Magruder
Sarah O. (West), 25
Thomas B., 25
Malloy
Ella Octavia, 51, 80
Jane Elizabeth, 83
Martha Elizabeth (West) Montgomery, 79
Martha Octavia (West) Davis, 23, 51, 80
Robert, 51, 78, 79, 80
Marion
Francis, 10
Martin
William T., 36
Maryland, 74
Mask
Esq., 75
Massachusetts
Boston, 29, 31
Massengill
Michael, 11
Masterson's Station, Ky., 6
Maverick
Samuel, 66
McCandless
Martha, 40, 41
McClutche
Isaac, 18
McCollum

Caroline (Neely), 44
McConnell
Dr., 85
McDonald
A. S., 66
McGuire
Joseph, 55
McMurran
John T., 36
McWhirter/McWhorter
George, 40, 42
Martha (McCandless) Balch, 41
Samuel C., 40, 42, 43
Mead
Cowles, Esq., 17, 43, 44
Mecklenburg Co., N.C., 40
Meng(e)
Elizabeth, 73
George, 72
Mary (-?-), 72
Permelia/Pamela/Paulina, 21, 72
Mirancy
E., 29
Mississippi, 8
Adams Co., 7, 14, 23, 25, 26, 35, 36, 41, 52, 75, 78, 80
Amite Co., 55
Black Hawk, 55, 56
Bolivar Co., 55, 81, 82
Carroll Co., 55, 56, 57
Church Hill, 76
Claiborne Co., 15, 35, 54, 73, 74, 75, 76, 78
Coahoma Co., 75
Cole's Creek, 33
Copiah Co., 79, 83
F. Stanton & Co., 72
Fayette, Jefferson Co., 45, 74
Franklin Co., 37, 52, 53, 54
Franklin Female College, 67
Greenville, Jefferson Co., 34, 40
Harland Creek, 63
Harriston, 74
Hinds Co., 63, 79
Holly Springs, 67, 68
Holmes Co., 29, 30, 31, 53, 54, 55, 63, 64

Seguin, Texas, 70
Seibe/Siebe
    Henry, 18, 39, 42, 86, 87
Seville, Spain, 12
Sicily Island, La., 29
Sillers
    Susan, 68
Simeson
    Simon, 3
Slocumb
    Charles C., Hon., 53
Smith
    John, 5, 6, 8, 21, 58
    John Jr., 5, 9
    Mary (Winn) West, 5, 7, 8
    Richard, 6, 9
    Zechariah, 11
Snedekar
    Garret, 2
Snodgrass
    John, 78
    Lydia (Swayze), 78
South Carolina, 9, 54, 58
    3rd S.C. Regt., 9, 10
    Camden District, 9
    Charleston, 10
    Chester Co., 10
    Columbia, 31
    Fairfield, 30
    Rangers, 9
South Carolina Rangers, 9
Southwestern University, 70
Spain
    Seville, 12
Speers
    Samuel W. (Rev.), 80
Spring Vale, Miss., 76
St. Tilla River. *See* Waterways, Satilla
    River, Ga.
Stampley
    William, 17
Stapp
    D. M., 66
Sullivan Co., N.C., 11, 26
Sullivan Co., Tenn., 11, 26
Sumpter's defeat, 10

Swayze
    Daniel, 30
    Daniel D., 29
    Gabriel, 78
    Lydia, 78
    Richard, 78
Tarrant Co., Texas, 83
Tchula, Holmes Co., Miss., 63
Tennessee, 10
    Bradley Co., 10
    Henry Co., 52
    Nashville, 27
    Rutherford Co., 52
    Sullivan Co., 11, 26
    Washington Co., 11, 26
    Wilson Co., 40, 42
Terry
    C. J. (Rev.), 31
Texada
    Manuel Garcia de, 13, 27
Texas, 68
    Austin, 70
    Bexar Co., 66
    Calhoun Co., 65, 66, 67, 69, 71
    Corpus Christi, 70
    Del Rio, 70
    Fayette Co., 69
    Galveston, 69, 70
    Houston, 70
    Lavaca Bay, 64
    Linnville, 64, 65, 70
    Port Lavaca, 65, 66, 67, 69, 70
    Ranger Cemetery, 66, 71
    Republic of, 64
    Rutersville, 70
    San Antonio, 70
    Seguin, 70
    Tarrant Co., 83
    Vasquez campaign, 65
    Victoria, 70
    Victoria Co., 64, 66, 71
    Washington Co., 70
Thomson
    William, Col., 10
Thornton
    John E., 69

Laura O. (West), 66, 69
Thrall
    Amanda (Kerr), 70
    Amelia (Trahern) West, 67, 69, 70
    Homer S., 67, 69, 70
Tichenor
    Gabriel, 59
Tilden
    Belle, 74
    Belle Tevis, 74
    Emily McIntyre, 74
    Marmaduke, 74
    Marmaduke Jr., 74
Tipton
    Mr., 29
Tolarsville, Holmes Co., Miss., 31, 55
Tomson
    Tom (enslaved by Wm. West 1769), 2, 3
Tonyn
    Governor, 9
Trahern
    Amelia, 21, 62, 64
    Delilah (Brashear(s)), 63
    Letha, 64
Trevilion/Trevillion
    Richard, 27
Truly
    James, 22
Tunica Co., Miss., 82
Turner
    Edward, 15, 16, 20, 28, 34, 35, 59
    Eliza. See Turner, Elizabeth (Baker)
    Elizabeth (Baker), 35
    Fanny Elizabeth, 36
    Henry, 36
    Lewis Ellzey, 34
    Martha Ann, 37
    Mary (West), 16, 20, 34, 35
    Mary Louisa, 36
    Nathaniel Lewis (1807), 36
    Theodosia (Payne), 34
    Theodosia Lavinia, 15, 35, 37
U.S. Senate, 14
U.S. v. Cato West's Administrators, 35
University of Pennsylvania, 58
Vandevall

John, 38, 39
Vaughan
    Susannah, 63
Vicksburg, Miss., 76
Victoria Co., Texas, 64, 65, 71
    Cornelius Lane & Co., 64
Victoria, Texas, 70
Villa Gayoso, Natchez Dist., 13, 38, 40
Virginia, 8
    Fairfax Co., 3, 7, 8, 21
    Fauquier Co., 5, 6, 8, 9, 22, 24, 41
    Frederick Co., 6
    Leesburg, 3
    Loudoun Co., 1, 2, 4, 5, 8, 11, 13, 21, 27
    Prince William Co., 3
    Richmond, 32
Washington Co., N.C., 26
Washington Co., Tenn., 11, 26
Washington Co., Texas, 70
Washington, Adams Co., Miss., 52, 77
Waterproof, La., 68
Waterways
    Arkansas River, 34
    Bull Run, 2
    Cedar Creek, Tenn., 11
    Cole's Creek, 13, 27, 33, 38, 39
    Holston River, 11
    Mississippi River, 11
    Nueces, 65
    Ohio River, 11
    Satilla River, Ga., 9
    Spring Branch, 2
Watkins
    W. Hamilton, 51
Webb
    Martha (Harper) West Davis, 19
    Robert, 19
    Robert [Jr.], 19
    Robert L., 19
Weedon
    Mary (Winn) West Smith, 6, 7
    Nathaniel, 6, 7
West
    Agatha M., 24
    Amelia (Trahern), 21, 62, 64, 67, 70
    Ann, 21, 30, 52, 62

Sarah Olivia (Dunbar), 25
Susan (by 1792), 21, 23, 50, 80
Susan (by 1792) (West), 21, 23, 50, 80
Susan C., 25
Susan Charlotte, 48
Thomas (1750), 2, 4, 8
Thomas (by 1787), 13, 16, 20, 27, 28, 38, 43, 58, 72
Thomas C., 25
Thomas C. (1861), 49
Thomas Cato, 46, 47, 49
Thomas Chinn, 24, 51
Thomas D., 76
Thomas Franklin, 75
Thomas W. (by 1787), 21, 22, 23, 24, 38, 50, 80
W. C., 25
Walter, 25
Walter Adrian Cato, 73, 75
William (1714), 1, 5, 7, 8
William (1782), 13, 14, 15, 20, 26, 27, 30, 62
William (1819), 16, 18, 19, 77
William Capt. (d.1761), 1
William H., 21, 86
William Howard, 25
William Jr. (1738), 3, 4, 5, 8, 12
William P., 31
William P. (1827), 31
William Parker, 32
William T., 24, 51
Willie. *See* West, William Parker
West Feliciana Parish, La., 23, 24, 51, 80, 83
Wethersfield, Hartford Co., Conn., 31
Wharton
  C. R., 75
Whitney
  J. M., 67
  Mary, 67, 68

Wilkinson Co., Miss., 23, 25, 50
Wills
  Martha, 12, 61
Wilson
  A., 51
Wilson Co., Tenn., 40, 42
Winn
  Ann (West), 21, 30, 52, 62
  Ann J. (Pate), 57
  Augustus O., 57
  James, 8, 9
  James E., 23
  John, 52
  John, Col., 11
  Joseph, 21, 52, 56
  Martha P., 56
  Mary, 4, 5, 7, 8
  Minor, 5, 7
  Minor Jr., 9
  Oliver. *See* Oliver Winn Phillips
  Penelope (Kirkland), 52, 53
  Richard, 9
  Samuel, 52
  Susannah Augusta, 56
Withers
  Benjamin, 22
  Sarah, 7, 22, 23, 41, 50
  Thomas, 22
Woodville, Miss., 24
Woodward
  Joseph, 52
Wright
  Elizabeth D., 31
Wyatt
  John D., Sheriff, 64
Yazoo City, Miss., 31, 32
Yazoo Co., Miss., 29, 53, 56, 62, 63
Yazoo Valley, Miss., 63
Young
  Robert Col., 26

www.ingramcontent.com/pod-product-compliance
Lightning Source LLC
Chambersburg PA
CBHW080338270326
41927CB00014B/3279